SINS OF THE MOTHERS

SINS OF THE MOTHERS

A MEMOIR OF ABANDONMENT, LOVE AND REDEMPTION

DONNA DAVIS

WITH AMY WILLESEE

Pan Macmillan Australia

First published in 2006 in Macmillan by Pan Macmillan Australia Pty Limited
BT Tower, 1 Market Street, Sydney

National Library of Australia
Cataloguing-in-Publication data:

Davis, Donna.
Sins of the mothers: a memoir of abandonment, love and redemption.

ISBN-13 9 78140503 7129.

ISBN-10 1 40503712 1.

1. Davis, Donna. 2. Orphans – Australia – Biography. 3. Mothers – Australia –
Biography. 4. Models (Persons) – Australia – Biography. 5. Female offenders – Australia –
Biography. I. Willesee, Amy. II. Title.

920.72

The names of all orphans and others in this book have been changed in order to respect
their privacy.

Typeset in 13/15.5 pt Granjon by Post Pre-press Group
Printed in Australia by McPherson's Printing Group

Papers used by Pan Macmillan Australia Pty Ltd are natural, recyclable products
made from wood grown in sustainable forests. The manufacturing processes
conform to the environmental regulations of the country of origin.

I dedicate this book to Harper, and to innocent children everywhere who may be neglected, mistreated and exploited.

PROLOGUE

A nurse comes into the delivery suite. Get up and have a shower, she says.

I can't, I plead.

Go and have a shower, the prison guard standing behind her orders me.

I think back to the births of my older children and how well the midwives took care of me. No one is caring now.

I stand to get myself to the bathroom but suddenly everything goes blank and I wake on the floor.

It's all right, Mrs Ehrenburg, you just fainted. The nurse helps me back into bed.

I am not well, I tell her, I'm just not well. I am crying and she must feel some compassion. She gently wipes my body with a warm cloth while tears roll down my face.

I am wheeled to the postnatal ward, to a private room. The two prison guards take up their post at the foot of my bed. They tell me that I might physically be in hospital but I am actually in jail; even though I have just given birth I am still a prisoner.

The next day I am allowed one visitor. My friend Leo Doublecross arrives, all yellow roses and brash confidence. Leo doesn't give a damn about the guards, he just looks at me and asks, So what do you want me to do?

Get me out of here, I say, as though that were an option.

Consider it done!

He is so confident, for a minute I feel as though I have a little bit of strength.

Truly, Donna, he asks, what else can I do?

I don't know what to do anymore, I say.

Where's the baby? he asks.

I haven't even touched the baby, I tell him.

I want to see the baby, he says.

I don't think that's allowed, I say.

But he is already manoeuvring me into a wheelchair and, flanked by the two guards, wheeling me down the empty corridor to the Special Care nursery.

My little baby is there in a humidicrib, nestled in his tangle of tubes. He doesn't make a sound. The guards stand over my shoulder as I search his features for something I recognise.

A nurse says it would help if I touched him.

I am too scared to touch this baby. Too scared I might love him and then have to let him go. The nurse gives him to Leo. Then Leo turns and places the child on my lap.

A surge of awe, love and fear swirls up inside me, so overwhelming I am almost paralysed.

In less than a minute, the nurse returns.

That's enough now, she says. We have to put the baby back.

She takes him from me and the tears come again. Uncontrollable tears. She must see how hard it is, because she turns back towards me and lightly takes my hand, guiding it into a gloved hole in the humidicrib. You can still touch him, she says.

His little chest heaves and jerks. His eyes are closed. He looks so fragile.

But reaching into the crib to touch his hand, I am shocked at

2

the strength with which he grasps my finger. So tightly that it jolts me out of my hopelessness.

And so, there in the Special Care nursery, holding hands and with the bleeping sounds of life support surrounding us, I make a pact with my child.

It's not going to be like it was with my own mother.

CHAPTER 1

My mother, Dorothy Warne, was the youngest of fourteen children. I suppose being the fourteenth child would make you a little eccentric – which is better than saying she was crazy.

The Warnes were a well-to-do family from Melbourne, Australia. My grandfather, Tom Summerhayes Warne, had been a great cricketer; they still have his bat and cap at the Melbourne Cricket Ground in remembrance of him. The Warne children were well educated. Except my mother. With her matchstick frame and black hair, she was an epileptic and because of this she suffered brain damage.

She was in and out of mental institutions because in those days that's where you went if you had epilepsy. Her family was ashamed of her, so they sent her to live in the country.

I don't know how my mother met my father, only that she tricked him into getting married. My father, William Davis, had just returned from Darwin, where he had been stationed with the artillery. My mother was already pregnant to another man when she met my father. The baby was called Ida but she was adopted by my mother's brother, who didn't know the little girl was mentally retarded.

My parents lived in a tin shed on a dairy farm in Gippsland, east of Melbourne. My father had grown up in a farming family on the Murray River. He could only write well enough to sign cheques but he was a good timber worker. Soon my mother was pregnant again, and again, and before she knew it she had Scarlet, June, Mary, Tommy, William, and another on the way.

My mother, being the way she was, had a habit of disappearing for days at a time. Apparently, she would go into town and go out with young men. She used to forge my father's signature and take his pay. One day he went to the bank and discovered all the money was gone.

Scarlet, at seven, used to take care of the other four when my mother went missing and my father was at work. Scarlet says she remembers giving six-month-old baby William water because there was no milk. One day she checked on him in his cot and found him very still. When the Welfare people turned up, Scarlet met them at the front door shouting, William isn't dead, William isn't dead, William isn't dead.

But William was dead.

So the four surviving children were taken away and that is how they ended up in orphanages.

I was still in my mother's belly.

I was born Lois Elaine Mary Davis on 15 July 1950. At the age of three months I was admitted to the babies' orphanage at Broadmeadows because of 'dietetic mismanagement' – and because the Welfare people said my mother was a semi-mental case.

I was left in my cot most of the time – except when I was in hospital with pains in my belly and problems with my bowel. I had weeping abscesses inside me that needed looking after; the doctors had to cut me open twice. They took a long time to heal, apparently. But I don't remember any of that. I only know about it because it is in my Welfare and hospital files.

My first memories are of St Aidan's Orphanage, north of Melbourne in the old goldmining town of Bendigo. The orphanage was big and dark, like a Gothic castle, with cellars below. The nuns swept by in black robes, revealing only their faces. Every time you approached a nun you said, Excuse me, and you bowed. Then you would hover, looking for ways to please, trying to be the girl who got to open the door for her. You called her Mother.

I always knew I didn't have a real mother.

I am five years old when I am called to the parlour. Only privileged girls are called to the parlour. Whenever you see girls leaving there, they are happy. I have never been one of the privileged girls.

I am handed over to a strange woman and told, This is your mother. She is taking you out for the day.

Gee, I have a mum. A mummy.

She is with a man who she says is my father but I don't think he is. We get into their lovely old car and when the girls see me they start shouting and waving, Lois! Lois!

Now I am someone really special. I am no longer an orphan.

My mummy has a bag of lollies. You never get lollies. As we drive down the long driveway, away from the orphanage, my mother winds down the window and throws lollies to the girls. I can see them laughing as they jump, trying to catch the treasure. I am smiling too.

I am taken to a big building. We go up to a room where my mother and the man she says is my daddy take off my clothes and put me on the bed. Then they tickle me. I can't remember anything else about this day. I just know I am naked and I am tickled. After that visit I don't see my mother again. Nobody explains why not and I never ask. I just don't see her and soon enough I forget I have a mother.

There are lots of girls who never have a mother for even one day.

CHAPTER 2

I can hear Mother Therese clomping around like an elephant. Her keys are rattling and there is thunder in her voice as she yells, Time to get up. The girls in the dormitory are sliding out of bed and onto their knees: Hail Mary full of grace the Lord is with thee blessed art thou . . .

Being a bed-wetter, I sleep on the verandah because I smell so much. Mother Therese has ways of knowing things, so, as soon as she walks onto the verandah, she knows I have wet the bed. She seems especially upset today as she whacks the strap across my bum. She knows just how to make it sting, and I cry and promise not to do it again. My wet nightie flaps against the sore bits and it burns.

Some mornings, Mother Therese wants to punish bed-wetters so she sends you to the isolation room or makes you stand outside with your damp sheets. She wants to punish me today.

After Mass she sends me to the courtyard and I have to stand there with my wet sheet over my head. The one good thing is that the whole sheet isn't soaked, so only my head and shoulders are touching the cold, smelly wee. The other girls march past me

9

on their way to school and I have to stand there so they can all see me. The girls circle around me and sing their song:

Mary Fishpot, Mary Fishpot

Lois Davis is a Mary Fishpot

I imagine they are my friends and they are singing, *Ring a ring a rosie, a pocket full of posy . . .*

Then the whistle goes for school so the girls run off, but I am sent to wash my sheets and put them through the wringer. I hang them over the fence and pray it doesn't rain because you do not want to have to go to bed with your sheets already sodden.

Mother Therese says I have to stand beside my sheets and I can't go to school until they are dry. But there is hardly any breeze today and even though I blow hot air on them and wave them about, they still cling to the iron fence. Eventually I pretend they are dry and make up my bed so I can go to class. I have probably already missed half the day but I don't really care.

The school is part of the orphanage and the nuns are our teachers. Mother Carmela is my favourite. She wears glasses and is petite and very gentle. I am her pet. Mother Carmela is in charge of putting shoes on our feet and she sees to it that I always get the best shoes. They are second-hand but I am the only girl who gets to choose my shoes because Mother Carmela likes me and it is very important to keep good feet, she says.

I am not one of Mother Therese's pets. Her pets are two sisters. They get to go to the Bishop's house for the Christmas holidays. But I don't think Mother Therese likes many other girls. She says she is going to come back and haunt us forever and she always walks around with the strap. Or a bag of lollies, which she eats in front of you. Girls grovel around, trying to get on her good side hoping for a lolly.

Mother Therese has whiskers growing out of her face. She is round with enormous breasts which she strokes constantly, even in class. She also has eyes in the back of her head. She walks around the classroom rubbing her hands up and down her bosom and holding her stick, looking in every direction for the chance to strike bare skin. Sometimes she uses a ruler. Not the flat part but the side, so she can get you with the sharp bit across your knuckles or the back of your legs. She drags you by the ear, too. One time a girl had her ear pulled and it ripped up the side. She had to have it stitched.

Sometimes I sit in class looking up at Jesus Christ hanging from the plus sign, which is what the cross looks like to me, and I think how much it must have hurt. I wonder if crucifixion would be worse than Mother Therese's stick. It looks worse. Other times I imagine what it would be like to burn in Hell, your soul on fire for eternity. Mother Therese says that I am going to burn in Hell. Sometimes I wish I hadn't been baptised because if you haven't been baptised you can't go to Hell, you go to Limbo. I would prefer to go to Limbo but since I have been baptised I will probably burn in Hell.

With all this thinking about the crucifixion and burning in Hell I need to go to the toilet but for some reason I can't put my hand up to ask. Mother Therese will give me a whack because I didn't go before class. So I just wee right there. It puddles on the floor under my chair. I put my feet over the wee, spreading it out, hoping to hide it. The other girls laugh and wave their hands in the air: Mother, Lois Davis wet her pants. There are so many trying to dob me in, they have to squeal to be heard. Mother, Mother, there's a puddle under her chair.

I get whacked and I have to clean it up but nobody ever makes me change my bloomers. We get a fresh pair when we have our bath on Saturday, although some days during the week my bum gets sore so I secretly wash my bloomers and sleep with them under my sheet to dry them quicker.

Ah, Lois Davis, you smell.

Girls don't gang up on me, they just don't go near me.

Sometimes I wish I could stick a bag over my private parts so I wouldn't be smelly and wet all the time. I wouldn't be Mary Fishpot anymore.

There are some men up on the roof building a giant television. None of us girls have ever seen a television before but the nuns reckon it is even better than the wireless. I can't imagine why they are putting it on the roof, though.

Finally, the workmen come down and everyone starts to get excited. I look up at the skinny metal thing on the roof and I can't wait to see what it will be like when they finally turn it on.

At four o'clock the announcement calls us to the hall to watch television for the very first time. I suppose the nuns must think there is a pretty good view from in there, but it is obvious to me that there is a much better view from the yard.

It is cold outside so I sit on the warm metal plate above the boiler room, with its excellent view of the roof. Another girl, Maria, joins me. Soon we can hear sounds coming from the speakers in the yard and, wow, this is it. We are really watching television. I can't believe the others are missing out on this.

Then a nun comes out and says to us, What are you two doing?

We're watching television, Mother.

You stupid girls, that's the antenna. The television is in the hall.

There must be a hundred girls in the orphanage. I am number twenty-two and when anyone calls twenty-two I jump to attention. You don't want to be disobedient, because then you might become a wayward girl and they will send you over to the other side to work in the laundry with the old women. Everyone knows you don't want to end up there. We are forbidden even to speak to the wayward girls.

Even so, there is something appealing about the wayward girls, so sometimes when we are at Mass we pass them love notes on the back of holy pictures hidden in our Bibles, and spy on each other to see who we like.

There are little boys in the orphanage, too, but they are kept hidden behind a fence. Sometimes I sit really close to the fence so I can secretly play with the boys.

We go to church each morning before 7 o'clock with black lace mantillas on our heads. We kneel in front of the altar for about an hour listening to the Mass, waiting to take the Holy Communion. Mother Therese says you must never ever touch the bread of Christ wafer. It goes straight in your mouth and you swallow it. You are not even supposed to chew it because it is the body and blood of Christ, but I secretly chew it anyway. It's yummy; if I could go back for seconds, I would.

Before my first Holy Communion the nuns told us about a little boy who hammered a nail through the wafer and how it bled and bled and bled, so be careful if you touch it. But I took it out of my mouth once and stuck my fingernail into it and it didn't bleed at all. It did nothing.

Sometimes when we are in the playground one of the girls points an imaginary gun at everyone and asks, Would you give up your faith if someone put a gun to your head?

And they all go, Noooo, nooooo.

Would you give up your faith, Lois Davis, if I put a gun to your head?

Of course, I am the first one to say yes.

Bang! Bang!

Mother Therese, Lois Davis wants to give up her faith.

Lois Davis, you are nothing but a pagan, a bad soul.

I run away to the top corner of the yard where I make a bed out of grass and leaves, and a soft grass pillow. Then I lie down and close my eyes to sleep, imagining that it is my very own bedroom and that I have a mummy who tucks me in and cuddles me.

As far as I know, I am alone in this world. The Welfare people have deposited us Davis kids into different institutions around Victoria, and nobody ever bothers to tell me I have brothers and sisters.

Sometimes I ask the nuns, Do I have a family? Where are my parents? The nuns should know because they know everything, but usually they don't answer.

Don't I have a mother or a father?

Your mother is an alcoholic.

I ask, What's an alcoholic? But they don't say. And, anyway, no matter how bad an alcoholic might be, I am sure it would be better than nothing.

I wish I could call someone mummy.

REPORT ON WARD	4.2.58
General appearance	Medium build, fair hair, blue eyes. Good complexion, good appearance.
Condition	Healthy child – but rather thin. Has overcome her bedwetting very much of late . . .
Persons interested	Mother has visited about twice since Lois was here, but child hardly knows her . . . No prospect.

Mother Therese won't let me drink anything in the afternoon anymore because she has had enough of my wetting the bed. I get so thirsty but there are spies all around so there is no way I can sneak any water. For a while, I don't wet the bed so much.

Each night before bed, we girls have to get down on our knees and pray. *I must die. I do not know when nor where nor how, but if I die with mortal sin I am lost forever. Oh, Jesus, have mercy on my soul.*

After that we cross our hearts and get into bed, me out on the verandah with the wind coming through the louvres. I lie there feeling the cold, my mouth dry as dust from having to clean my teeth with salt and nothing to drink since three o'clock. Even though I try to suck the moisture from my toothbrush, it is not enough. My lips are sticky with thirst.

I lie there forever, waiting for everyone else to fall asleep, trying to think of ways to get water. I wish I could escape to the bathroom.

What if I get caught?

Who cares.

So now everyone is asleep, I slowly creep out of bed and sneak to the bathroom. I sit on the toilet and squeeze out every last drop of wee, and while I am straining I make up my own prayer: *Please God deform me in any way but don't let me wet the bed.* Over and over again. *Please God deform me in any way but don't let me wet the bed.*

My mouth is so dried out. I sit there wondering, Do I do the unthinkable? I stand up and close the door properly. At least now no one can see me. Then I get down on my knees over the toilet bowl, flush the chain twice and on the third flush I drink and drink and drink. I use my hands to scoop the water up to my mouth, and it tastes great. I feel disgusting but it is so refreshing, I don't care. I guzzle until I am not thirsty anymore.

The whole way back out to the verandah and back into bed, I repeat my mantra. *Please God deform me in any way but don't let me wet the bed.*

My eyes want to close but I try hard to stay awake. If I don't fall asleep, then I will not wet the bed.

Of course, I do fall asleep, and when I wake up in the morning, the bed is wet again. Not that it stops me from sneaking to the bathroom to drink the toilet water that night, and the following night, and the night after that. All the time repeating my prayer over and over. It never works, though. I think God mustn't listen to pagans.

Some nights when I tippee-toe to the toilet, the girl who is in charge of the bed-wetters is still awake and she stops me. She is not a nun, just an older girl who mustn't realise she is allowed to leave.

As I am creeping past, she whispers, Lois, come here. Come over to me.

I walk over to her bed.

Now get on your knees, Lois.

I kneel down beside her.

Give me your hand.

I give her my hand and she pulls it under the blanket and rubs it against her private parts. She shows me how to move my fingers and I do what she wants. The nuns make us cross our hearts before we go to bed so that we don't play with ourselves but they don't say anything about playing with her. And, anyway, I do whatever she tells me, because when she is finished I am allowed to go to the toilet.

Mother Therese is very disappointed that I am still wetting the bed so she sends me to a psychiatrist to put a stop to it. The psychiatrist gives me some medicine that is supposed to stop bed-wetting, but it doesn't.

So one day, Mother Therese says, We are going on an excursion to the zoo tomorrow, but if you wet the bed tonight you will not be going and you will have to stay here on your own.

We never go on excursions so this night I sit on the toilet forever repeating my mantra, *Please God deform me in any way but don't let me wet the bed*, and squeezing out every last drop. I don't even drink the toilet water because I would rather be thirsty than miss out on the zoo.

When I wake before dawn the next morning the bed is wet. I lie still in the one comfortable spot where my body has made the bed warm, not wanting to move because the rest of the bed is so cold I will freeze. I am so used to this feeling of lying in a warm wet bed. But then I have a brainwave. I hop up and quickly swap my sheets with the sheets from a spare bed, hoping and praying no one wakes up and sees me because I will be dobbed in for sure. When I am finished, I crawl back under the lovely dry covers to wait for Mother Therese to wake us up.

I didn't wet the bed, Mother! I didn't wet the bed!

So, she says, how do you explain the puddle under your bed, Lois?

I guess I'm not so clever after all.

Get up to the isolation room.

I have to write I will not wet the bed, I will not wet the bed, one hundred times. But I know I will wet the bed.

So I don't go on the fabulous excursion and instead I have to sit on the stairs watching the good girls getting on the bus. Never mind, I've got my eye on the loquat tree instead. That will be my outing. As soon as the bus has driven down the driveway, I sit under that tree and eat its yummy little sour yellow fruits.

I spend the afternoon alone playing jacks with five small stones. If you are lucky you can have jacks made from knuckle-bones, but five stones is good enough for me. I build myself a grass bed and fall asleep imagining I have a family.

I am used to being alone, anyway. I am not someone you would want to make friends with or get close to because I don't talk very much and I always have a big stain on the back of my dress.

At breakfast we eat bread and dripping or porridge. Sometimes on Sunday you get an egg and even a cup of Corn Flakes, while the nuns always eat eggs on toast. You are not allowed to see a nun eating but I know what they eat because Marlene, who works in the kitchen, gives us their crusts if we're lucky. We all wait for her to bring them in her apron outside and drop them on the ground. Girls push to get to them first.

I love those crusts and I always eat breakfast because that's okay but I hate lunch and dinner. Sometimes I chew the food then spit it out again, but sometimes I can't even touch it. Mother Therese and Mother Claire walk up and down behind our benches with big metal spoons and if you don't eat you get whacked on the head from behind. I get so many whacks on the head. Eventually they hold my nose and force the food into my mouth.

After a while, I work out that it is easier to hide my food. First I try putting it in my cup and turning the cup upside down, but I get caught doing that, so then I start spooning it up the sleeve of my jumper and into my pockets. Or I chew it up then spit it down the front of my top. You have to be really sneaky, and I am.

When I get outside and I am sure none of the other girls are around, I scrape the food out of my clothes. I smell so disgusting with wetting my pants and the food in my jumper that no one goes near me anyway.

Ah, Lois Davis, you smell.

Even I can't stand the smell of myself but I can't get away from me.

*

Sometimes I get hungry at playtime so then I dig in the ground looking for bobbies. Bobbies look like tiny little bean sprouts and taste very sweet. Occasionally you get a yucky one but I love my bobbies.

Other times I sneak peas and beans from the garden when we are meant to be picking fruit and vegetables for the nuns. That is one chore that we like. You have to fill your apron with peas, and if you come back and your apron isn't full they know you've been eating them. I manage to sneak some anyway. The peas are really yummy.

On Saturdays, after Mass and scrambling for crusts, we scrub the floors and the walls. I am the best floor-scrubber. And we wash the cupboards and polish the silver. The nuns eat with silver. Also, we have to darn our socks and knit our jumpers. I might be stupid, but I am good at knitting. I am also good at swimming and often win prizes.

The best thing about Saturdays is that we have our bath and get a fresh set of clothes and underwear, so for a while I don't stink. You line up for the bath and there is a nun there saying, Quick, quick. You have to keep your underpants on the whole time because otherwise you might touch yourself and that would be a mortal sin. Everyone uses the same face washer and towel and bath water – if you are lucky you are first but, of course, I never am.

Late in the afternoon we line up in the courtyard for nit inspection. You kneel with your head in a nun's lap and she scrapes and pulls through your hair looking for nits. If she finds any, she cuts off all your hair. The nuns seem to love hacking off your hair and I always have nits, but certain girls seem never to have nits. Like Jane. She is so holy and clean. She wins prizes for the best made bed and is always getting privileges. Jane has beautiful long, black curly hair.

But one day Jane is caught putting a moth down the back of Francesca's dress. Mother Therese drags Jane to a bench in the middle of the courtyard and we all crowd around while the nun hacks off her hair. Jane is sobbing while the nun holds her thick black curls up in the air for us all to see.

Sometimes Mother Therese gets really mad when you've got nits so after she has hacked off your hair she locks you under the stairs in total darkness. There is only enough room to sit down and it is full of cobwebs and smells horrible. You have to sit there until she lets you out.

An even worse punishment is when Mother Therese waits until very late at night and then calls out the names of any girls who have been naughty that day, or maybe of girls who wet the bed. If your name gets called, you have to go outside one by one to receive your punishment.

Mother Therese is sitting in her chair in the courtyard and she tells you to walk around the entire orchard by yourself. It is pitch black so Mother Therese can't see you but she has ways of knowing if you have walked right the way around. You can't go too fast because then she will say you didn't do it and make you do it again. You can't go too slow, either, because then she will say that you have been getting up to mischief.

Sometimes I get all the way around, running and crying through the darkness as I try to escape the monsters hiding in the shadows, too scared to look back because maybe I will turn into a pillar of salt just like Lot's wife in the Bible. But some nights I only get as far as the centre and freeze. I stand there sweating and wetting my pants until eventually I work up enough guts to return to the courtyard.

I often wonder if she could do this to you if you had a mother and father or brothers and sisters.

*

Some nights I have a dream where I am found guilty.

All the nuns are there in their black robes. My punishment is death. The rope goes around my neck and they hang me. I can't breathe. All this white stuff, like foam, is pouring out of my mouth. I try to take it out but more appears.

There is no one there to save me.

You wouldn't tell anyone about the dreams because that might be putting ideas into the nuns' heads.

One morning I wake from this dream to the sound of keys rattling. The bed is wet. It seems to really bother Mother Therese today. She sends me and the three other bed-wetters to the isolation room to get the strap and says, You will never wet the bed again because tonight you will die.

So after school that day we have to go to Mother Therese's office to die. We each stand in a different corner and Mother Therese locks us in and leaves without saying a word. We are supposed to stand, but as the light fades we sit and we stand and we sit. When we think someone is coming, we stand.

I never speak to the other girls. For hours we are silent in our own fear. I sweat and cry to myself, imagining what it will be like to die at the hands of Mother Therese in the dark.

I wonder how she is going to kill us.

Then we hear the keys in the door and I am wetting my pants, sweating so bad, and all I keep thinking is, I hope it's one of these other girls before me.

Mother Therese opens the door. Our time is up.

She walks in and turns on the light. Go to bed, she says.

Nuh, this is a trick. She is going to get us. This is just a trick.

She follows us up the stairs and I wait for her to get us from behind. We walk faster and faster, looking over our shoulders, waiting for her to strike. But by the time we reach our beds, Mother Therese is gone.

*

I am too scared to tell anyone but I've got sores all over my bottom and between my legs, and every time I wet my pants, it burns. In class I have to sit with my bum pushed right into the hollow at the back of the seat so that I am not sitting on my sores. Washing once a week might be okay if you don't wet your pants but for a smelly thing like me it doesn't help the sores on my bum.

My favourite nun, Mother Carmela, must finally notice that I am in pain because she asks me what is wrong.

Nothing, Mother.

You're walking a bit funny.

I've got sores on my bottom, I finally say.

I show her and she looks shocked.

Please don't tell anyone, Mother, I'll get in trouble. (I don't want to get whacked on my sores.)

She agrees not to tell and instead comes up with a plan. She arranges for me to be the blackboard monitor, which means that twice a day I get to take the blackboard dusters outside to clean. Then, while I am out of the classroom, she says, I am to run quickly to her room and knock on her door.

When I knock, Mother Carmela quietly takes me up to the yard – I think she is worried that Mother Superior will find out what she is doing – and I lie on the bench with my pants down and get some sun on my sores. Mother rubs ointment into my skin and it stings but feels nice at the same time. Then I have to rush back to class.

Eventually I can't keep it a secret, though: the sores get so infected that Mother Carmela says I have to go to hospital.

I lie on stiff green sheets and there is a blinding light overhead. The doctor squirts some stuff between my legs then slices off the sores. I scream so much they have to hold me down.

But at least I get to stay in hospital for a week.

REPORT ON WARD   14.7.59

General appearance   Average build, very thin child,
                      appears delicate & below par at
                      present
Condition   General health – poor. In hospital
                      with boils recently.
                      Has had mumps.
                      Enuretic?* Yes, regularly.
Education   Grade III
                      Position – Low
Behaviour   Normal, slow speaking . . .
Persons interested   No visitors
General comments   Not a very bright child

*Enuresis: involuntary discharge of urine, especially while asleep

I am eleven when Mother Therese calls me to the parlour and
tells me I have a sister. No, no, it's not me, I say, you've made a
mistake. I haven't got a sister.

Yes you have, says Mother Therese, her name is Scarlet, and
she is coming to visit tomorrow. But if you wet the bed tonight I
will cut off all your hair and you won't be allowed to see her.

I know they have made a mistake because I am an orphan,
which means I don't have any sisters, but now suddenly the
other girls all want to talk to me. Lois has a family. A sister. And
it starts to sink in. I am like one of the privileged girls. Should I
get excited about this? Am I really not alone after all? I can't wet
the bed. What do I do?

I sit on the toilet. *Please God deform me in any way but don't let me wet the bed. Please God deform me in any way but don't let me wet the bed.*

I am not going to drink the toilet water tonight.

CHAPTER 3

I fight against sleep for hours before finally drifting off.

But when I wake the next morning the bed is cold and wet.

I feel lost. Everyone knows that if the bed is wet I am not allowed to see my sister.

So what.

I go about my daily chores. And I don't see this Scarlet. Nobody says anything. It isn't mentioned.

I wonder what she looks like.

I wonder if she is even real.

The following day, Mother Therese calls me to the parlour. Standing there is an older girl I don't recognise.

Lois, this is your sister, Scarlet.

Oh, she is beautiful. Eight years older than me, and much darker. She has the prettiest long black curls and angelic looking features.

Mother Therese is standing behind me.

Lois is a lovely girl, she tells my sister. She is very happy here, aren't you, Lois?

Mother Therese pinches my upper arm hard, with a smile.

You're happy here. (Another pinch.) Aren't you, Lois.

Oh yes Mother, I say, I am very happy here.

It is afternoon already, so Scarlet and I only have a short time together. We sit in the garden and she tells me how she spent ten years at an orphanage called Nazareth House, a couple of hours away in Ballarat. She says I have another sister, called June, who is still there. Scarlet left when she turned seventeen. It has taken her a while to find me because the Welfare wanted to protect my privacy so she had to ring every orphanage until she found me. With me being so young, why I wasn't put with my sisters is beyond me. Scarlet says our mother is a horrible woman and if she ever contacts me I should stay away from her, but that we've got an Auntie June and more aunties and uncles, and another sister called Mary who used to be at Nazareth House, except she had epilepsy and one of her fits worried the nuns so they sent her to a mental institution, never to be seen again. Poor Scarlet tells me she used to watch Mary constantly because if she fitted, Scarlet was the only one who knew what to do.

I've got a brother, too, Tommy. He used to be right here at Bendigo until he got too old and had to go to St Augustine in Geelong. I wonder if he was one of the boys I used to play with through the fence when I was little.

Family at last. I sit there admiring Scarlet's beauty. There is so much to absorb and remember so I can go back and tell the other girls every detail. Question after question – you can't slow me down. I want all the answers now.

Scarlet says I was the only sibling she didn't know, me being the last child and taken away from my mother soon after birth. She says my birthday is the fifteenth of July and that you have a birthday every year and she is going to send me a present for my next one. Only kids who are visited have birthdays. Orphan kids don't have them.

Scarlet says that you can tell we are sisters because we have the same thumbs. Skinny at the bottom and square at the top. Murderer's thumbs, she calls them. Scarlet knows so many things.

She tells me all about the orphanage she was in and how there are five different schools in Ballarat you can go to, so every morning you get to leave the orphanage and catch the bus to school. And how Sister Peter is really nice and she lets you have long hair. It sounds like a dream and I want long hair so badly. I ask Scarlet if I would be allowed to go to her old orphanage with our sister June and she says okay, she will try to arrange it for me.

That night I guzzle the toilet water and I don't even care if I wet the bed because I've got a family, I am not alone anymore. I feel like a flower going from winter to spring.

The Welfare people have told the nuns that I am too skinny, so now each day after school I am sent to the kitchen. I have never been in a kitchen before and the first thing I see is a big bowl full of speckled eggs and a pot of fat potatoes. Mother Seraphina is a frail old nun in charge of fattening me up and she thinks I am the ant's pants. She doesn't usually get to spend time with any of the girls. Come with me, Lois, she says. Sit down. She makes me egg flips and cakes and I feel like the queen of the orphanage.

I wait and wait for the fifteenth of July to come around. My birthday. All the girls are excited because I know when my birthday is and that must mean I am someone special. Oh, Lois, they say, you're lucky it's your birthday. None of the other girls know when their birthdays are. Some of them even think I'm lying. You can hear them: Mother, Lois Davis is telling lies.

Even so, in the playground that day I have so many friends.

Mother Therese is standing there with her bag of lollies, so I tell her that it is my birthday.

How do you know that? she asks me.

My sister told me.

Here you go, she says, and hands me a black jelly baby from her treasured lolly bag. Now everyone is jumping around me, important Lois, and calling out to Mother Therese. Mother, Mother, when is it my birthday? When was I born?

Mother Therese laughs, As if I would know when all you girls were born. Even though she supposedly has ways of knowing everything.

I carefully divide my little black jelly baby into pieces to share with the other girls. Half a head to someone, half a head to someone else. An arm to one, a leg each, and then there's the body, which goes a long way. I have part of the body and I keep that little bit on my tongue for nearly the whole afternoon.

I am eleven and playing on the swings in the yard of the orphanage. Suddenly I lose my grip and I crumple to the ground, crying. My left arm hurts really badly. And there is blood. My elbow is bleeding. One of the older ladies who looks after us, Kath, says it doesn't look good and takes me to the hospital. The doctor says it doesn't look good, too. He tells Kath that I have a fractured arm and then he bandages it up.

Kath takes me back to the orphanage. The bandage feels too tight and my arm is aching awfully for days and days, but I can't tell anyone because then I will have to take a dose of castor oil.

When Kath takes me back to the hospital for a check-up, my hand is all puffy and swollen. The doctor looks at it from different angles and squeezes it a few times. Then he bandages it up again and says it will get better but it never does.

After that, my left hand is weak.

*

Now that I have a sister I get one or two letters in the mail each year. Scarlet writes that she is trying to have me transferred to the orphanage at Ballarat, but in the meantime, the Christmas holidays come around and I am sent to stay with a family who want to look after an orphan for a couple of weeks. They live on a farm and I get to milk the cows, and you don't get whacked for wetting the bed and the lady says I can call her Mummy if I want. I do; I want to call someone Mummy more than anything. So I'm all the time, Oh, Mummy! Mummy! Until one of the daughters snaps, She's not your mother.

Scarlet doesn't seem to be having any luck with the transfer because I am still at Bendigo when it comes time for my confirmation. The nuns make us new white dresses and Bishop Stewart confirms us and afterwards we have coffee and biscuits in the parlour. If only we could be confirmed every week.

We get to choose a name for our confirmation and I choose the name Therese, hoping Mother Therese will like me for it. I race to tell her, Mother, Mother, I've chosen a name! I've chosen Therese!

But she is very busy; she isn't interested.

REPORT ON WARD	15.3.62
General appearance	Tall, very thin child with straight fair hair & green eyes
Condition	Physical condition – Swollen cervical glands, boils . . .
	Mental condition – Retarded
	Enuretic – Yes, even during day
Behaviour	Not difficult

<u>Education</u>	Grade V. Conduct – Average. Progress: V. slow.
<u>Persons interested</u>	M/. never visits, whereabouts unknown F/. " " " "
<u>General comment</u>	Lois asked if there is any possibility that she could be transferred to be with her sister . . .

CHAPTER 4

I am nearly thirteen by the time Scarlet comes to take me to Nazareth House. My other sister June has already left there but I still want to go. I would go anywhere just to leave St Aidan's. I imagine that my life is about to begin. I will go out to a real school and no one will know I'm called Mary Fishpot. I will be able to have long hair.

I think we take the train but I don't really remember. Only that I feel quite excited but still a little strange around my sister because I don't really know her. She seems to want to help me, though. She keeps saying, You'll like it at Nazareth House, you'll like Sister Peter, she's really nice.

When we arrive at Ballarat, the first thing they want to do is cut my hair. Which really annoys me. Scarlet said I could have long hair. So I appeal to Sister Peter but uh-uh. Sister Peter is not the Sister Peter I was hoping for. Scarlet must have been her pet because she wants to be a nun but I am not going down that road.

So they cut off my hair.

Oh, well. Ballarat is still pretty nice compared to St Aidan's. It is brighter and the food is better and there is no laundry where they send wayward girls. Someone gives me the nickname Cuppity, after the Davis Cup, because I am Lois *Davis*, and Cuppity is much better than Mary Fishpot. I get on a bus each morning to go to St Alipius School – the pleasure of going out on the street – and we learn to speak French. *Au nom du Pere, du Fils et du Saint Esprit . . . In the name of the Father, the Son and the Holy Ghost.* Religion again but at least it sounds better in another language.

I am amazed, too, that the orphanage lets you have music lessons, and you even get to choose your own instrument. Cello, piano, violin, drums. So I choose the piano, because I have always liked the idea of playing the piano. Each Tuesday a tall man with dark hair comes to the orphanage to teach piano. Apart from the priest and the gardener back at St Aidan's, he is the only man I know. He teaches me to read music and always says, Keep your hands on the keys, Lois. Keep your hands on the keys.

The best thing about Nazareth House is that nobody knows I am a bed-wetter and even if they did, it wouldn't matter because they don't beat you for it. The mattresses must be better quality than at St Aidan's, too, because the wee doesn't drip through and make a puddle on the floor. Sometimes you don't even have to change your sheets.

Plus, the girls all want to know the new girl from the other orphanage.

A girl called Beverley introduces herself. And I think, Oh, there's a girl with that surname at St Aidan's. Then more girls introduce themselves and there are more familiar names, and I realise, well, if I had three sisters in Nazareth House, of course there must be other girls who have sisters, too. Suddenly I feel something inside me snap. Have the nuns really known this all along and never said anything? Even if they don't know, the Welfare knows, that's for sure. We may have no mother or father, but the least they could do is let us have each other. Soon word gets around that the new girl knows who has family. For the first time I have a little bit of power, and it feels good.

Out in the yard, girls come up to me. Lois, do I have a sister?

And what is your name? Yes, you've got a sister, Betty, actually, in Bendigo. You look like her.

So then these girls go to the nuns and say, Lois Davis says we have a sister in St Aidan's. And the nuns say that I am causing problems. Some of the girls even decide they are going to run away; hitchhike to Bendigo, knock on the door, and find their sisters. It's my fault for unsettling the girls, but I don't care.

Scarlet is living in a bungalow in Dandenong and her landlords are called Mr and Mrs Huer. Scarlet says they can't have children, so she takes me to meet them and tells them they can have me if they want. Scarlet says it is most important to get me into a good family.

The Welfare says I can spend weekends with them while everyone decides whether I should be adopted. Mr and Mrs Huer are very kind, and they must be rich because they give me new toys and my own room and tell me that if I come to live with them, they will buy me a brand-new bike and put me into the best school in the district. The only bad bit is the food. German food. I'm only used to eating orphanage food and I don't even like that. Plus, I'm not used to being on my own. But the weekends are nice anyway.

Then the Welfare tells Scarlet that because I am thirteen, it is going to be my choice if the Huers adopt me or not. So Scarlet says to me, If these people adopt you, you will never have any connection with the Davis family again. You will never see me again. You have to understand that. You'll lose that.

I think about this over and over. I want Scarlet so badly it aches inside me and in the end I say, No, I'd rather live in an orphanage.

So I stay at Nazareth House and my sister decides that she doesn't really like me anymore. She tried so hard to find me a family and it was a big responsibility and now I won't take the family that she has given me.

> Whilst at Ballarat on 18/10/1963, I was informed that Lois Davis is getting on fairly well at Nazareth House. Her sister, [Scarlet], visits regularly, the last time two weeks ago. [Scarlet] is going to Sydney at the end of November and may take employment there.
>
> W.R. Hughes
> O/C CHILDREN'S HOMES

One Tuesday afternoon I am having my piano lesson when the teacher puts his hand on my leg. Keep your hands on the keys, Lois, he says. Then the next week he touches my leg again, but this time he moves his hand further and further up my skirt.

Keep your hands on the keys, Lois.

He fiddles around with me. It sort of feels good at first but then it doesn't.

I let him do it each Tuesday and each time I am thinking, No, no, no – but I can't move, I can't speak. I am too scared of this man. So then I decide the piano is not for me. The nuns don't ask why, they just let me quit.

I can't understand this place where nuns don't want you to

know your family, and where sisters go off to Sydney and don't visit you anymore, and piano teachers give you strange feelings. I feel so weird inside. I just want to escape it. I have to get out of here.

CHAPTER 5

I ask to return to St Aidan's. Scarlet has obviously given up on me, and at least Mother Carmela is at St Aidan's. So, just before my fourteenth birthday, I take the train back to Bendigo.

I have changed so much since I left. I am not going to be docile Mary Fishpot anymore, no way. So, it isn't long before I am in trouble. I swear at another girl, pull her hair and kick her. I don't know exactly what she has done or said to annoy me, I just know that I am not going to put up with that same old stuff.

Mother Therese washes my mouth out with soap and tapes my lips shut. Then she tapes my wrists and my ankles together. She says this is so I can't swear or hit or kick anyone else. The tape stays on all day and only comes off for mealtimes. I am not allowed to talk, just eat, and then the tape goes back on. The nuns all say this isn't like me. They can't believe how troublesome I have become, what a foul mouth I've got. Even Mother Carmela can't understand why I am causing so much bother.

What's happened to you, Lois? she keeps saying. You have to try and be a good girl.

I just say, There are all these girls who have sisters and nobody tells them.

But how do you know that?

I know them, I say. It's true. Look at me, my sisters were there. It's not fair. Why do they separate families? We don't have a mother, the least you can do is let us have our sisters.

She doesn't say anything after that.

St Aidan's has changed, too, since I have been away; for some reason the nuns have decided that we don't have to go to church seven days a week anymore if we don't want to. They will settle for three or four days, but it is up to us. Well, I'm not going to church every day if I don't have to, no way. So I go three times a week even though most of the other girls still go all the time. The nuns call me a pagan and tell me my soul will burn in Hell.

So why did they change the stupid rules then?

One morning I wake to find that my cold wet sheets are stained red. There is blood and pee everywhere. I go berserk, crying and yelling, I'm dying! I'm dying!

Mother Therese bustles out to the verandah, keys jangling. What in God's name is all this fuss about? she asks.

I'm bleeding to death, I cry.

Whack.

That shuts me up.

Mother Therese is angry at me for drawing attention to this revolting mess. She says it is supposed to be a secret and it is just the filth of the body working. Then the girl in charge of the bed-wetters who makes me touch her privates takes me down to the cellar. It has no windows and she says I mustn't tell anyone about it. She hands me some rags and says, You have the curse and you're going to have it every month.

I don't know what she is talking about, this curse, but it sounds bad. She says that each time I have the curse, I am to come to the cellar every day after school, and she shows me where to wash the rags and hang them out to dry. Never tell any-one about this, she says.

So now I have a secret. Some girls who obviously don't have the curse yet ask me about it but I tell them I can't say.

<table>
<tr><td colspan="2">REPORT ON WARD   10.11.64</td></tr>
<tr><td><u>General appearance</u></td><td>Slim, rather delicate looking girl with straight fair hair, blue eyes, fair skin (rather rashy).</td></tr>
<tr><td><u>Condition</u></td><td>General health – good
Illnesses – had 'flu during winter
Whether enuretic – Yes, has fin-ished her Tofranil tablets</td></tr>
<tr><td><u>Education</u></td><td>Grade VI
Progress – retarded
Prospects (vocational) – Would like to be a hairdresser.</td></tr>
<tr><td><u>Behaviour</u></td><td>Rather troublesome – inclined to be sly (Sister).</td></tr>
<tr><td><u>General comment</u></td><td>Lois asked where her father is. Is anything known in Head Office? An appointment will be made at the Bendigo Base Hospital for visit to psychiatric centre.</td></tr>
</table>

Because I have reached a certain age, Mother Therese says it is time I learned about the birds and the bees. I line up outside her office with all the other girls of a certain age and in we go one by one.

38

Mother Therese is sitting at her desk and I sit across from her. She shows me a drawing, which she points to with her pen and says, This here is a penis, and this is a vagina. The penis goes in the vagina and that is how you make a baby. It is a mortal sin to do it before you are married. Okay, send in the next girl. *Next*!

We all laugh about it afterwards. It's pretty funny.

We get the chance to see a real-life penis one night when a girl standing at the upstairs window calls out that there is a man down in the courtyard taking off his clothes. We rush to the window to look while the nuns run around in a panic shouting at us to turn the lights off this instant. One of the girls is downstairs and the naked man, who we nickname Charlie, asks her for a fuck. But she doesn't know what a fuck is so she asks the nuns and they give her a beating and lock her under the stairs.

In the end, the police come and take the man away. Apparently, he escaped from the mental hospital in Bendigo. So that is our first viewing of a naked man, although I don't see anything. Even some of the nuns must be interested in boys because they get excited over them when we are watching TV. Mother Philomena likes Elvis Presley and Mother Claire likes Roger Moore. He's in *The Saint*. They let us watch *The Saint* but sometimes they yell, Close your eyes now, and we all have to close our eyes. I never peek but I'm sure the nuns do.

I have never been especially interested in boys, but something has happened, something has changed.

I find myself looking forward to seeing Father Duffy. You can't just go up and talk to Father Duffy alone – he talks to all the girls but only in a group. So I find myself trying to get to the front row in Mass, trying to sit as close as possible to Father Duffy so I can see his face and watch him closely. I try to get his attention, wanting to be more revealing around him, to be prettier than the other girls.

Whenever it is time for confession, I wish that it is Father

Duffy in there – not Father Owen. But then Father Owen is killed in a car crash and after that it is always Father Duffy at confession. I am kind of happy about that, in a way.

Going to confession means I can have Father Duffy all to myself, away from the prying eyes of the nuns. He blesses me, talks to me, hears me. Sitting in that little booth, he opens the black curtain and I steal looks through the screen at his profile. I tell him about my sins and my bad thoughts. Not that I ever let him know that these bad thoughts have anything to do with him.

I find myself thinking of him constantly. Thoughts come into my mind that I don't understand; feelings coming from somewhere new that have nothing to do with education or God. I know it is wrong to have these thoughts, but they stir up such beautiful feelings and sensations. I am amazed that someone can cause you to feel like this, that my body is revealing something to me. Something is awakening in me. I don't understand it exactly, but I like that this is something I have for myself – my own secret feelings that the nuns can't control, can't take away from me.

I tell Father Duffy that I'm having these strange feelings, I'm having bad thoughts about somebody. I tell him that I've done things with a girl. I will say anything just to be with him. Sometimes I ask him, Is it a mortal sin to have bad thoughts?

I feel a bit naughty, cheeky. But in a nice way. He blesses me and gives me my penance. Then my time is up and I have to leave my private sanctuary with the handsome Father Duffy.

The other girls wonder why I go to confession so often: She must have committed a lot of sins. But I don't care.

Anyway, you can commit any crime you want, so long as you say the act of contrition.

*

Someone has taken a handle off one of the cupboard doors and Mother Therese thinks I did it even though I know for a fact it was Maureen.

It was you, wasn't it, Lois, Mother Therese says.

No, Mother, I didn't do it.

You're a liar, Lois Davis.

No, Mother.

Well, Lois, a parcel has arrived for you from your sister but until you admit that you took the handle off the cupboard, you are not going to get it.

I want that parcel so bad but I am not going to admit to something I did not do. So I get a belting and Mother Therese tells me that when I am ready to own up to taking the handle, I can have my parcel.

Weeks pass with no parcel so Mother Carmela finally has a quiet word to me. Why don't you just say you took the handle and you can have your parcel, she says.

But I didn't do it, I say.

Just tell a little white lie, Lois, she says. You've already been punished for it, and then it will be over and you will have your present.

So I say I did it and Mother Therese gives me the parcel. It is a Christmas present from Scarlet. A watch. I am the only girl in the orphanage with a watch and am so excited when I've opened the parcel.

I am fortunate to have a sister who sends me a watch but I still wish I had a mother. The nuns are getting sick of my incessant questions. All the time, Where is my mother? Where is my father?

Mother Therese says, Your mother is wicked.

I want a mother so bad it aches inside me.

I wish I could get to the outside world. Escape this feeling, this place. I just want to run away.

We go for walks up One Tree Hill or to the cemetery to look at the headstones of nuns and ladies we once knew. We have to be very quiet. No speaking or you will wake the dead. Mother Carmela walks in front of us girls and Norma, the nun's helper, walks behind. I walk next to Norma and, wherever we go, I look for ways to get out, to run away. We are at the cemetery one day when I decide, This is my chance.

I pick my moment and make a run for it. Norma is yelling out, Lois, Lois. Don't go! Come back! Where are you going to go? What are you going to do?

Where I'll go doesn't enter my head, I just run. Running down the street like a marathon runner. I can run so fast no one will catch me.

I hide in the bushes for a while and then I go into Bendigo, to the supermarket and all this incredible food I've never seen before. The lolly section. I take what I can and stuff it in my mouth. I expect I am a criminal now. I keep looking over my shoulder, waiting to get caught. Then, of course, it gets dark and I have no money and nowhere to go. It's not like someone is going to take me in, with me wetting the bed. I suppose there will be a missing persons report out on me anyway, so I decide to call the police and give myself up.

My name is Lois Davis, I say, and I'm on the run.

The police take me back to St Aidan's, where Mother Therese gets hold of me. She locks me in the isolation room, saying, Where were you? Where were you?

She is obsessed with the thought that I have been having sex with boys.

Tell me where you were, she says.

Just hiding in the bushes, Mother.

No you weren't. You were with boys, weren't you?

No, Mother, I was hiding in the bushes.

You're not leaving the lock-up until you tell us where you were.

42

All right, I was with boys, I say.

She is happy then. Oh, she was with boys. So, I get strapped for that and locked up anyway. A girl is put in charge of me, waiting to dob me in if I even think about running.

I spend the whole time planning my next escape. I have to be careful about it, too, because if you are naughty enough they send you to reform school. One of the other girls, Carol, ended up in a reform school.

The next time we go on a walk I promise not to run. We go to the cemetery and, of course, I make a run for it. I hide behind a headstone until everyone is gone and then I just wander the cemetery for hours. Going around looking at how old people were when they died. The Catholics have their own section. It starts to get dark and I am scaring myself with all the headstones but I keep telling myself I am not going back. I am never going back.

But in the end I find a phone box then ring the police.

My name is Lois Davis and I am on the run. I want to give myself up.

REPORT ON WARD	11.5.65
General appearance	Tall thin girl with rashy face, straight fair hair and blue eyes. Anxious expression and rather abrupt manner.
Condition	General health – Usually good. One sore throat.
	Whether enuretic – Is en. On Tofranil – attends BBH Psychiatric Clinic
Education	St Aidan's.
	Progress not good – retarded.

<u>Behaviour</u>	Very unsettled when she returned from Nazareth House. Is happier now.
<u>If family member, location of and contact with siblings</u>	[Scarlet] – sent watch for Xmas. No contact since. [Tommy] (with [Scarlet]), never sees. [June] and [Mary] in Melbourne – never sees.
<u>General comment</u>	Ward asked if [Scarlet]'s whereabouts could be discovered? Is anything known in Head Office?

I am starting to worry about what the nuns are planning to do with me. Mother Therese says I have no prospects. This is my last year of school because only the clever girls go to high school and I am not one of those lucky clever girls or a favourite. Mother Therese says I am mentally retarded. I suppose most of us are mentally retarded, as only two of us are going to high school.

Lucky girls get to go out into the world, and that is everyone's dream. That's what we talk about, going out into the world. Sometimes you wake up in the morning and one of the girls has disappeared, never to be seen again. No goodbyes, no chance to stay in contact. The nuns never say where she has gone, we just know she's gone out into the world. Wow, how lucky is she.

Sometimes I wonder, How do they pick certain girls to leave? Nobody has ever said that I can leave. No one is going to take someone who wets the bed and won't eat her food. So the way I see it, the only option left is to send me over to the other side to work in the laundry with the wayward girls and old women. But I really, really don't want to go over to the other side because once you're there, that's it, you just work until you die. You never get to go out into the world.

So I think, what does it matter, and I swear at a nun, because the nuns – or something – just make me so angry and I don't want to be treated like a bloody idiot anymore, a Mary Fishpot. I don't really even know what fuck means, I just know it's a swearword, but telling a nun to get fucked is a mortal sin so I am dragged kicking and screaming to the other side.

CHAPTER 6

```
┌─────────────────────────────────────────────────────┐
│                                                       │
│          REPORT ON WARD            30.6.65            │
│                                                       │
│  General appearance   Tall thin girl with wavy fair   │
│                       hair, blue eyes and rashy skin. │
│                       Withdrawn manner.               │
│  Condition            General health – good.          │
│                       Whether enuretic – No.          │
│  Education            Prospects (vocational) – Packing│
│                       room half day.                  │
│  Behaviour            Came from other side of Convent │
│                       yesterday due to difficult      │
│                       behaviour. Absconded once,      │
│                       negative in attitude to almost  │
│                       everyone (Sister).              │
│  Persons interested   Nobody visits or writes.        │
│                                                       │
└─────────────────────────────────────────────────────┘
```

I am now over on the other side where you get old and die. Except now that I am here, it's actually not so bad. Some of the wayward girls are even talking to me. They can't believe how young I am, being sent here to work and having no family. They give me so much attention, asking what I have done wrong. I tell them how I told a nun to get fucked, because I don't care who knows about it. They say that I must have done something more than that because everyone here has done much worse; they have all been in trouble with the police. And I say, No, that's all, so then they feel sorry for me because I am just an orphan with no prospects.

The nuns are different on this side, too. It's not like they are training you because you are already trained. You belong with the wayward girls now, the old ladies. You don't have to eat your dinner, and if you wet the bed, who cares? Nobody complains, no one whips you, you just have to wash your sheets, hang them on the line and go to work. Too easy.

They put me to work in the laundry's packing room under Nellie Dusting. At first I think, My God, they have handed me over to a madwoman. Nellie is this huge old lady with whiskers growing out of her chin and her cardigan buttoned up wrong. She's all the time talking: Lois is going to help me, Lois is going to help me. Pacing and rubbing her hands together and dribbling as the words pour out of her mouth faster and faster. Lois is coming, Lois is coming. I'm going to be in charge. Lois is coming. I'm your friend, Lois Davis. I'm your friend.

She is a bit disgusting but funny at the same time. I like her. She is at least kind to me. She takes me by the hand and drags me everywhere.

I ask her, How long have you been here, Nellie?

I've been here all my life, all my life. Since I was a baby. I've been here all my life.

Now I know this is the end for me. I am going to end up like Nellie Dusting.

Anyway, I like working in the laundry. It is an enormous

47

room filled with washing machines and dryers and big rollers where they put the sheets. The laundry trucks come in each day with the dirty clothes and linen from other orphanages and boys' homes. Where I am in the packing section there is a long table, and it is my job to fold and sort each boy's clean clothes into piles. I might be retarded but somehow my brain grasps this really well and I can remember all the boys' names and where their piles are and I can throw the clean clothes into the right pile without even having to look. Getting everything done in record time. And, wow, there's even music, the radio crackling out these brilliant songs I have never heard before. Dusty Springfield, 'Wishing and Hoping'. And I dance around the table, imagining I am on stage as the girls in the rest of the laundry watch me running from one end of the room to the other, throwing clothes at different bundles. So I act it up even more and Nellie praises me for doing such a great job and the nuns all go, My God, she is amazing.

One of the old ladies is dying. Nellie Dusting sits with her in the infirmary while the rest of us, every chance we get, sit outside the door and wait for her to die. Each afternoon, lunch break and weekend we are there, fascinated, straining to hear something until Nellie emerges to give us an update.

Nellie appears at the door like a performer on the stage. We snap to attention and there is a hush as we wait for her news. She knows we will hang on her every word, and she enjoys a few extra moments to rub her hands, her grey whiskers twitching as she grins.

She's got three days to live, Nellie finally announces. I don't know how she knows that but she has experience with this sort of thing.

The next day, Nellie reappears on her stage outside the infirmary door and reports, She's losing her eyesight. She's losing her hearing. The hearing's gone. The eyesight's gone. Two days to go.

On the third day, Nellie announces, She's got the death rattles, she's got the death rattles. After that comes the news, She's starting to smell. Now we know she is near the end because we realise there is a certain order to death.

After that comes the long silence, only broken when Nellie starts screeching. She's dead! She's dead!

The nuns are called to the infirmary and all shuffle inside. Nellie keeps us informed: They've straightened her out.

Then: They've plugged her up. They've stuffed up all her orifices. Now they're going to wash her.

I don't know what the hell they are going to wash her for when they are just going to bury her.

When she is prepared, they put her in an open coffin in the church and we all have to put on our Sunday clothes and line up to view the body. The nuns go first, then the old ladies and us wayward girls, then the orphan kids. Some of us say goodbye, some of us file past, silent. Part of me thinks it's a bit disgusting, but the other part really wants to touch her to see what she feels like. You're not allowed, though.

Afterwards, we go to the cemetery to bury her. Everyone looks forward to that. It's an outing. We chatter and laugh until we reach the graveyard, where we're not allowed to make any noise. Shhhhh. I don't understand why, because they wouldn't be burying her if they thought she could wake up, would they?

No one from outside ever comes to the funerals – there is only us.

Mother John dies next. She dies of cancer. Nellie says that when you die of cancer you go black straight after death. I don't know whether it's true or not, because we aren't allowed to see Mother John's body.

It is like an old people's home on this side of the convent.

Everyone waiting to die and us waiting to take their place. So after the novelty of working in the packing room starts to wear off, I am definitely thinking that I don't want to stay here. Some of the older girls put it into my head that the nuns have no right to keep me here, anyway. You've never committed a crime. You can leave. Not that I have anywhere to go.

I go to a nun and tell her that I want to leave. She laughs at me. Where are you going to go?

I want you to find me a home, I say.

Yes, we will do that in three months time, she says. We will find you a home.

But three months pass and nobody says anything about it. I am convinced they have no plans to let me go out into the world and I start to get depressed. Even Nellie says to me, You're never going to leave. This is your home. What do you want to go out for? Look at what you've got. You've got a job, a bed, three meals.

Lying in bed at night, what Nellie has said starts to frighten me. I can't stop thinking about how to get out of here. I go back to the nuns and ask them to find me a home. In three months, three months, three months, they keep saying. I think, Nuh, I'm never getting out.

I can't wait any longer. I don't know what is going on inside me. I am so unhappy all of a sudden. I feel like my insides are screaming out but no one can hear me. I can see I am either leaving here in a coffin or my way.

I tell a couple of the older girls about my plan to escape but I think they think, Oh yeah, sure, little Lois Davis is going to escape. Even though other girls do escape sometimes. Generally speaking, you double your time if you escape, but I don't have time to double because my time is forever – what does it matter?

The gates are kept locked but I have discovered that you can sneak out through the laundry when the trucks are pulling in. So, the first chance I get, out I go, bolting down the driveway and repeating in my mind, Never look back, never look back. Just keep going.

I run down St Aidan's Road, as far as I can, not knowing what else to do. I've got nowhere to go but I'm too scared to go back. I hide for a while but it soon becomes obvious that I'm too stupid even to run away properly. In the end, of course, I call the police again. I'm very official about it. My name is Lois Davis and I am on the run. I would like to give myself up. They come and get me, put me in the back of the police wagon and return me to the convent.

Once I'm back there, though, the same fears continue to eat away at me, so I keep running. The police keep bringing me back. After a while I'm such a nuisance that the nuns have to take some drastic action. They decide I am to wear nothing but a singlet and underpants to work in the laundry. They know I won't run away in a singlet and underpants. My skinny body is there for all the girls to see. You couldn't humiliate me any more but I don't care.

I just long to escape this feeling of imprisonment. It is overwhelming.

I am fifteen when one of the nuns comes up to me in the laundry and tells me my mother is here to see me. Oh, you've got the wrong Lois, I say. I don't have a mother.

No no, she says, she is here for you.

No, you've made a mistake. I am panicking. No way.

There is no mistake, she says. You have to come with me.

All right.

So I follow her to where this woman is, and she is with a man who is a bit crippled. The nun says, This is Dorothy, your mother.

I look at her black hair and her pathetic, skinny body and I

51

just think, No way. She is not my mother. They are not my parents.

I say, You have made a mistake.

The woman speaks up. You're Lois Davis?

I nod.

Then I am your mother, and this is your father.

I turn to the nun in alarm. I feel scared and I don't know why. I don't want to leave the grounds, I tell her. I don't think I'm allowed to leave with her. You don't know the whole story.

The nun says okay, and instead I sit outside with them and we talk. The woman is chain-smoking Camel cigarettes and slobbering like a mad person, and every revolting thing about her makes me ill. She is supposed to have been a beauty in her day but I can't imagine that. It turns out she has come to see if she can take me out of the orphanage so I can work for her. She is strange, my mother. I feel so utterly ashamed.

I had always imagined that if I had parents they would be wonderful.

CHAPTER 7

The Director of Family Welfare,
P.O. Box 2765 Y,
MELBOURNE, C.1. VICTORIA

17th February, 1966

Dear Sir,

Lois DAVIS, born 15.7.50

The abovenamed is said to be a ward of your Department. She absconded from St Aidans Good Shepherd Convent, Bendigo, early in February with another girl named Sonia . . . and arrived at her sister's home . . . She and her companion were accompanied by two youths on the journey interstate. She denied that she had misbehaved herself in any way on the journey. The girl said that she had absconded from the Convent as she had been working in the laundry and did not think she would ever be released . . .

Would you please indicate if the child is a ward of your Department and whether you desire her return to your care.

Yours faithfully,

(A.C. Thomas)
UNDER SECRETARY
Department of Child Welfare and Social Welfare,
New South Wales

I just want to see Scarlet. I don't know where I am going, only that she is in Sydney. So Sonia and I hit the road.

We meet two boys in Bendigo with the same surname as me. They are called Davis and I am called Davis. They are thin and I am thin: I decide they are my long-lost brothers. They are nice boys; they can probably see how innocent we are. They feed us and take care of us on the long drive to Scarlet's. (Even after they leave us in Sydney, one of the boys sends me letters which he signs, From your loving brother. They are love letters in a way, beautiful letters from someone kind. No one has ever written letters like that to me.)

The boys drop us at Scarlet's house in Blacktown – well, down the road from her house. I can't have her see me get out of a car with boys. But she isn't home.

It's just Sonia and me, on the run together, and we are going to stick together. Only we have nowhere else to go. We are lost. Where will we go? Who would want us? I know I have an older brother, Tommy, somewhere nearby. Scarlet wrote to me about how she got him out of his orphanage and set him up in a boarding house not far from her. I have never met him before but I have his address from Scarlet, so we decide to hitchhike and try to find him.

A carload of boys picks us up – I don't know how many, but they say they can help. Get in the car and we'll take you where you want to go.

So we get in the car and they drive us around, take us to a house. Somehow I am led into a room – I don't know exactly how, but I've gone into a room, and there is a single bed. I don't know where Sonia is. She's disappeared.

This could be my room. It looks like a little girl's room, a single bed against the wall. Somehow I end up on the bed and the boys are taking off my clothes. I am naked.

There are more boys in the room now, maybe five or six, but still no sign of Sonia. Maybe she is in another room. I don't know what's happening to her, but awful stuff is happening to me. I've never in my life felt this. It's hurting me, this long hard thing being rammed inside of me like I am a piece of meat. I am frozen with fear, too scared to do anything. I can't move, can't get out. All these things are happening and I am scared – lost, desolate, empty.

People, telling me things. You've got to move, girl, move. Move ya bum. Move. *Move!* Oh fuckin' hell, I don't know what's happening, what I'm supposed to do. That one's finished, It's my turn – hurry up, hurry up! The door is opening and closing. Another one comes in – and I am lying on the bed scared out of my wits.

I don't know what you call this. I don't even know what rape is, what it means. I am a virgin. I have never seen a naked man before this day. I never have a choice, I never even know I have a choice. I want Scarlet so bad but I know if I tell her she won't believe me. How can I tell anyone?

It is over and somehow I get out of the house. I don't know

what has happened to Sonia. I wonder if she knows what has happened. She might have run away if she is smart enough. Or she could have left me on my own, I don't know. Maybe she didn't get hurt. Maybe it was just me. She has disappeared.

So I am just standing there on the road and I can't move. I am sore and this stuff is all dripping down my leg. What have I just been through? What has just happened? God, who can help me? Where do I go? I'm on the run. Do I cross the road? Do I go right? What do I do? Scarlet? Mother Carmela? Somebody please help me. I want a mother. Any mother will do.

I am sobbing now, really feeling sorry for myself. So hollow, so ashamed.

It's not like I can go to the police: I am on the run, no one is going to believe me, understand me. I can't go to Scarlet, I am too scared to tell her. I decide to find Tommy.

Tommy is very gentle and quiet and I say to him, These boys have done all these things to me. I don't know what to do. I am crying, sobbing. But he just gives me this confused look and doesn't say anything, except, Oh.

He only left his orphanage a month ago and he has never been with a woman so he can't understand what I am saying. He doesn't know how to advise me, what to do, what to say. Just, Oh.

We know as much about the world as each other. We're lost. And that's when I feel, There really is nobody. I am on my own. No one cares what happens to me. No one is interested.

So Tommy and I separate, and I don't see him for years after that. We don't know to contact each other. When you've had no family, you are really emotionally retarded. When the nuns said I was retarded, they were probably right in a way.

I go to Scarlet's place and she doesn't want to talk about what happened with the boys. She gets me a live-in job with a family, but it only lasts one day because I wet the bed. So then Scarlet asks me, What do you want to do?

I tell her I want to be a hairdresser, so she gets a piece of paper and she says, All right, I'll test you to see if you can be a hairdresser. You need to draw a straight line.

I draw a line and Scarlet says, No, that's not straight enough. You can't be a hairdresser.

So I can't be a hairdresser. All right, I say, I could work in a laundry. I'm good at laundry.

But I think Scarlet can't help me anymore because she phones the Welfare and dobs me in.

[Handwritten note in Welfare file]
22nd February, 1966

. . . If the girls do return to Victoria Sister does not want them back at St Aidans. Sister was very disappointed in the girls. When Lois turned sixteen she had a typing job ready for her. Lois seemed to be unsettled since her mother visited around Xmas time.

TELEGRAM
Directress
Good Shepherd Convent
Victoria St,
Ashfield, NSW

Re. Lois DAVIS. REGRET DELAY ARRANGING RETURN. FLIGHT 407 TAA BOOKED FOR 21-6-66 EX SYDNEY 1.10PM. CHILD WELFARE SYDNEY WILL CONTACT YOU RE ARRANGEMENTS.

They fly me back to Melbourne, which is pretty groovy, I suppose. I wear my one and only outfit, which consists of a black and white striped cotton dress, blue woollen coat, white handbag and shiny black shoes. All hand-me-downs from the nuns. And I sit there looking out the window, wondering how they keep this thing in the air; what freedom it is to fly. They ask me on the plane if I want some lunch but I say no, because I only have $3.58 and I don't know how much it costs. Then I see everyone else is eating this food like it is heaven and my mouth starts to water, and I realise that you don't have to pay for it. I really want some now but it is too late. Stupid woman, she should have told me it was free.

In Melbourne I am taken to Winlaton girls' home. The nuns mustn't want me back. They have given up on me; I have gone too far this time. I really have. After what happened in Sydney, I feel dirty and horrible. How much worse can I get?

I have heard other girls talking about Winlaton. It is a reform school, and a reform school is almost as bad as going to jail. That's where they come at you with broomsticks. Only young girls who have committed a crime go to Winlaton. I wonder if I have committed a crime.

How long will I be here? I keep asking.

The woman in charge says she doesn't know. Your case is a little different, she says, because you are from the orphanage. You might have to stay here until you are eighteen because you don't have a home.

That would be two years. No way.

They fill in some forms, take my belongings and send me through to the other girls. I know straightaway that I am out of my league here. There are bars on the windows and guards at all the doors. Every room you enter is locked behind you. Now for sure I can't get out. The girls are nasty, yelling at authority and at each other. Fighting constantly, and violent, too. I have not seen violence like this before.

I am doomed.

I stand against the wall, too scared to talk to anyone or even move around this place. At least the girls don't come near me most of the time. Ha, she's just from the orphanage. Leave her alone.

For once luck must be on my side, because after two weeks Mother Claire agrees to take me in at Oakleigh Convent in Chadstone. Mother Claire used to teach me in grade three at St Aidan's so she has decided to give me a chance. I think Mother Carmela asked her to help; she was horrified when she heard I was in Winlaton.

So I am transferred to Oakleigh, another convent with another laundry. I work in the laundry, but this time always with the promise that I am going to leave soon. At least now they know how desperate I am to be put with a family. *Find me a home, find me a home.*

YOUTH WELFARE DIVISION

15.7.66

Lois seen at Oakleigh on 13.7.66. In interview Lois was rather withdrawn & covertly resentful of being a Welfare girl & spending all her life in institutions. Although Lois did not volunteer many of her feelings & attitudes, she agreed as her feelings were verbalised for her. Initially she was very wary and impressed as a girl who could be very difficult . . .

It is just that whole feeling of there being no escape. No way out. I do try to behave myself, especially for Mother Carmela's sake.

She writes me letters asking me to please be patient. She says that one day I will go out into the world.

But the waiting is too much at times. I can't stop thinking of Nellie Dusting. I am like her. Exactly like her. Months go by with no one finding me a home and I realise I am never going to get out.

I give Oakleigh six months before I nick off again.

This time I have an address for Jane, the girl with the beautiful hair and manners from back at St Aidan's. Mother Carmela secretly told me where she was: she has a live-in job with a doctor's family. So I go there and she takes me in for a few days, hiding me in her room so the family never sees me.

Gosh, what a lovely house. Doctors must make a lot of money. Jane even has her own bathroom. She has got it made.

Sometimes when the family is at home it gets too risky and Jane makes me get under her bed. But then when everyone goes out Jane has charge of the house, so I can come out and she cooks for me and we can talk.

Jane says that the first week she came here, the doctor made a pass at her. She says the first time he kissed her she had an orgasm. Jane must be very sexual. She was worried that she would fall pregnant because that was what the nuns used to tell us, but she didn't. You have to go the whole way for that to happen.

After a few days, Jane packs me off with some food. I head into town and wander round the shops. I look at the food halls and the pretty clothes and bras. All the girls at Winlaton wore bras. Back at St Aidan's, developed girls only wore bodices, which are like a bandage strapped around you so you look flat. Jane wears a bodice. She is very developed. She says because they are so tight I'm lucky I don't have to wear one. I am a very slow developer. No breasts and no hair under my arms. But I am dying to wear a bra.

I haven't got a clue what size I am. Too many styles to choose from. Any bra will do, so I pick a white one, nothing fancy, and take it into the dressing room.

I put it on under my blouse and walk out of the shop. It is a little big but I feel pretty good. I wonder if anyone can tell I am wearing a bra. Then someone grabs my arm and obviously he can tell I am wearing one because I am busted. I have to go back to the shop and explain myself. But I think they must realise I am not a normal person because they just take the bra back and let me go.

Not that I have anywhere to go, so I phone the police myself. My name is Lois Davis and I am on the run from Oakleigh Convent. I want to turn myself in.

They pick me up but Mother Claire doesn't want me back at the convent. She says there is nothing to be gained by taking me in again.

So it is back to the steel bars and broomsticks of Winlaton, with me just trying to melt into the walls for six long weeks before they try to transfer me to another convent. But uh-uh, I am not going through all that again. If I want a home I am obviously going to have to find one myself. So, on the drive to the convent I make my escape.

I am on the run for two weeks before I turn myself in to the police.

Another institution . . . eight days, this one lasts . . . I make my escape . . . but there's nowhere to go . . . I turn myself in . . .

And back to Winlaton.

Good Shepherd Convent,
Bendigo.
March 29th, '67.

My dear Lois,

It was only to-day I heard that you were at 'Winlaton'. I know it was what you most dreaded but never mind dear, if you really try this time to be good, it will be the last time.

I write tonight to beg you to try and do as you are told, not to be rude and impudent to those who are caring for you. Just try to convince yourself that those people like us, just want to help you to make good.

I know how difficult it is to do the right thing when you are in the company that you must mix with there. I have heard other girls who were there, say how hard it is to try and hold out against other girls, but no matter how hard it is Lois dear, promise me you will try. It is entirely for your own sake I beg you to promise me this.

... There is just another thing I would like you to promise me Lois. Do not let them tattoo you. Put up a big fight against it won't you? It will be so hard to get a decent position later on if you are tattooed and it costs so much to get rid of it if ever you can . . . .

God bless you dear. Keep your chin up and don't forget to say your prayers. Tell your God you are sorry for everything. He will forgive and forget as soon as you do. You know that.

I am, dear Lois,
Yours sincerely,
Sister Carmela

I can't do it. I feel so desperate. I cannot stay in this place. I wake up each morning and I breathe it every minute of the day, there is no escaping it. I just want to be out in the world, walk alone in the streets and not look over my shoulder. But even if I could walk out freely, where do I go? What do I do?

I am trying to be good. I miss Bendigo, Mother Carmela. I need help. Someone? Please help me. Get me out of here. I am going to go crazy if I don't get out.

I am taken into the city for a doctor's appointment, and as soon as the van pulls up at the kerb and that door is open, I bolt. Faster, faster, faster, I am saying in my head as I sprint across the street. I am good at this by now. I duck into a pub on the corner and hide in the bathroom. I sit on the toilet listening to my heavy breaths. I sit there for I don't know how long, it seems to be forever, and only leave once I am sure the coast is clear.

I hitchhike out of town and end up in Queensland, where I must do something wrong because I get dragged into children's court. I don't remember much except that they send me to a convent in Ipswich – another institution – on the grounds that I am living under conditions that indicate I am likely to lapse into a career of vice or crime.

Is that what they think?

The girls at Ipswich listen to The Doors and The Kinks and The Who. I am only there a week or so before I run away and hitch back to St Aidan's to see Mother Carmela.

She is not expecting me but I have it in my head that St Aidan's is my home. I can go there whenever I want.

Lois, what have you done? she says. She looks disappointed in me.

I tell her I want to stay with her in Bendigo. I beg her to help me, not to give me up. She hides me in the isolation room over the weekend and sits with me for hours, telling me to be good and have patience, but we both know that come Monday she has to notify the authorities. By law she has to, and even though she likes me she is not going to break the law for me.

The only thing she can do is help me write a letter to the boss of the Welfare.

Good Shepherd Convent
St Aidan's
Bendigo

Dear Mr Thomas,

Well I suppose the last time you heard from me was when I was in Queensland but as you can see I am now in Bendigo. I ran away from the Institution in Queensland because it was my eleventh Institution and I am just fed up with them all. I know it is my own fault . . .

I know that jobs aren't that easy to get but if you do get me one, I would like a living in job in Melbourne, but if I have to stay here until you get me one could you get my clothes sent down to me. Miss Mundy said she would ring up Chelsea House and see what she could do.

Yours faithfully,
Lois Davis

P.S. My clothes are all at Winlatten.

St Aidan's
Bendigo

Dear Mr Thomas,

Well as you can see I am writing a few times again
hoping you are in the best of health because I don't feel
too good at the moment after what Mother has told me.
Mr Thomas could I go to Abbotsford instead of
Winlatten. Please, I don't want to go to Winlatten
because I know I will come out of there worse than what
I come there.

Every time I give myself up to the nuns I am always
put back to Winlatten and I am just fed up with them all.
Could I go to Abbotsford for a few weeks until I get the
job please.

Yours faithfully,
Lois Davis

P.S. I promise you this time I'll be good if you just get me
out of Winlatten.

The Welfare people take me back to Winlaton anyway.

A week before my seventeenth birthday I run away again.

But this time I know I am not going to give myself up – and
after my first night alone, I never wet the bed again either.

CHAPTER 8

Suddenly I am out in the world, only nothing has prepared me for it. I don't even have a place to live.

Another girl who has run away arranges for me to meet a boy named Graeme Thomas. She says he and his mate will take me to a shack in the country where I can stay for the weekend.

So we head to the bush and when we arrive, Graeme wants to have his way with me. I start to think that might be the only reason he brought me here. But it doesn't take him long to realise that I am just out of a home and it is obvious I am too scared to have sex with anyone, so he can't do it to me. He doesn't even try.

After that, Graeme decides he likes me. I have never had anyone after me before and Graeme seems nice enough. He is very handsome. He is the same age as me but he seems older. He drives a Zephyr – he's into his cars and his mates – and he wants to look after me. He arranges for me to live with his sister for a while and gets me a job working at the Heidelberg Dry Cleaners.

Graeme is in love with me, I guess. He is always ringing me at the dry cleaners or waiting for me outside after work. I don't think I have that feeling towards him, whatever that feeling is.

But we start dating anyway and after a long while I do have sex with him. It is at his sister's house and it is not terribly romantic. I don't even know what to do. Then afterwards, Graeme is angry because he says he can tell I am not a virgin. He says I have been with other men.

Boys are able to tell these things, I suppose.

I don't explain it to Graeme. I don't want to talk about what happened in Sydney. He is still my boyfriend but now that he knows I was not a virgin he will never marry me. After that, I decide I don't want to stay at his sister's house anymore. I would rather get a live-in job with a real family.

Lois Davis came to work for me on the 25th July 1967 and we arranged on the wages of Twenty Dollars per week and full board. There is two days off each week and one week's notice given by either party.

Mrs J. [Kristian]

Graeme helps me get the job with Mrs Kristian. We find it in the paper. I lie and tell her I am eighteen so she won't know I am on the run from the state.

Mrs Kristian is a single mother with bright red fingernails and hair to match. She is thin as a twig and always wears high heels and caked-on make-up. I move into her house and at last I have my own room, just like Jane. Mrs Kristian is pretty well off for a woman on her own.

I have to look after her two kids, who are aged three and four. I don't like kids much. Nobody does, I guess. At the orphanage everyone said they were a nuisance, babies especially. I have to cook for the children, so Mrs Kristian shows me how to boil a potato and fry up a sausage. I am not great in the kitchen. One thing I am good at is cleaning the house. Scrubbing floors and washing sheets. I have it down to an art, and I will do anything just to be free.

Every night, Mrs Kristian goes out and doesn't come home until three or four o'clock in the morning. It's quite good because it means Graeme can come over and we can hang out. Sometimes we go into Mrs Kristian's room and look through her things, which is Graeme's idea. One night we look through her underwear drawer and find a stash of money. Hundreds of dollars. Maybe thousands. I can't stop staring at it. After that we go in there every night and count it. We always put it back exactly where it was. We are just amazed because we have never seen so much money. Graeme says Mrs Kristian is a prostitute for sure. You get a lot of money for that sort of stuff. She probably only has to have sex once for my whole week's wages.

Now that I am out on my own with a live-in job, I have the opportunity to meet more of my family. Scarlet introduces me to my other sister, June. Those two grew up in the same orphanage and have our mother's dark hair. When I meet June for the first time, there is no overwhelming revelation that, Wow, I have a sister, the way there was when I first met Scarlet. But June is very warm and immediately I take it for granted that we have a bond; that even if we don't know each other yet, we are in this together. I feel a great need for family and so I latch on to her.

With my family ties slowly beginning to blossom, I decide I want to see my mother again. I have her address on a piece of paper she gave me when she visited me at the laundry, but I am terrified to visit her on my own. Scarlet has warned me about her. Scarlet has a real thing about our mother because she was there when she let baby William die. Don't ever find our mother, she says. She's dangerous. June says the same. Be careful, she says. She'll chase you. She'll hit you. In our minds, our mother is the wicked witch. But there is something in me that wants to see her anyway.

Just in case anything happens, I take Graeme with me. I don't care what Graeme thinks.

I find her living in a boarding house in Mary Street, St Kilda. I am too scared to go in so I call from the door.

Come on in, she says.

No, I'm fine here, I say.

Even from the front door I can smell her. Stale and poor and old. I am so ashamed. She is sitting there with her legs open and her dress pulled to the top of her thighs. Horrible skinny legs. She's sucking on a Camel cigarette. She is disgusting, scary.

I can't bring myself to touch her.

I vow never to speak to her.

Graeme thinks I am pregnant; I have not had a period for a couple of months and my clothes are starting to tighten around my waist. Jane arranges for me to see her boss, the doctor, and he confirms it. I am about three months along.

Graeme says we have to decide what to do. He thinks we should tell Mrs Kristian and see what she says.

So we tell her, and Graeme and Mrs Kristian come up with a plan. Mrs Kristian says I should keep the baby and that she will cover my medical expenses – obstetrician, private hospital and all; that she and Graeme will swap cars; and that she will give me some money once the baby is born. In exchange, I will have to visit the doctor in Mrs Kristian's name and book into hospital in her name. She will keep the baby.

I suppose I wouldn't know how to take care of a baby, and

Graeme and Mrs Kristian both think the plan is a good one. Graeme says that, in any case, no one will let me keep the baby, me being an orphan. He says the baby will be taken from me. And Mrs Kristian says I can't stay living with her if I don't agree to their plan and I will be back out on the street. I am a ward of the state until I turn eighteen and there is no way I am going back to Winlaton.

So I go to the posh doctors on Collins Street and pretend my name is Mrs Kristian. My tummy blows up like a balloon and soon I can feel the baby fluttering inside me. I know that being an unwed teenage mother is nothing to be proud of but the more I think about the baby, the more I wonder if maybe I wouldn't make such a terrible mother after all. For some reason I keep thinking it is going to be all right.

I am about six months pregnant when I tell Mrs Kristian that I have changed my mind. I want to keep the baby. Mrs Kristian says that if that's the case then I have to leave.

Graeme finds us a bungalow in Thomastown and we move in together. He is never going to marry me, though; he is strict about that.

He works as a painter to pay the rent, but because I can't cook and am not aware of my domestic responsibilities, Graeme stays away a lot. For some reason I become very emotional about this and it is only a matter of weeks before Graeme tells me I have to go.

I don't have any feelings for him, but I still don't want to be chucked out. He's someone to hang out with.

But I am back out on the street, with nowhere to go. The baby is due in a couple of months and I have no job, no home. Just a little money saved up. I won't have the private hospital and obstetrician now, obviously. I don't know where else to go so I hitch down to Heidelberg and Graeme's parents. I turn up on their doorstep unannounced and tell Graeme's mother I have nowhere to live. I ask her, will she help me since I am carrying her grandchild?

She says she doesn't want to be involved. She thinks I should leave.

I plead with her but she tells me to go away.

I had sort of hoped that maybe she could be my mother. But she didn't warm to me at all.

I walk up to Ivanhoe and hang around the bowling club. I meet a couple of girls from West Heidelberg and spend a lot of time with them, or with girls from the orphanage and friends of Graeme's. I float between houses and anywhere that will have me. Wherever I can get a bed. I don't tell anybody that I have nowhere to live. They all think I am just staying the night and then going back to Mrs Kristian's.

During the day, I wander the city until I am exhausted and I have to find a bus stop to rest my legs. Or I go to the lounge at Myer's. The department store is a good place to hang out because they have television and a comfortable lounge, a toilet and even a telephone. It's as though it is my own lounge room. People there come and talk to me: How are you? How long have you got to go? No one suspects anything. And I usually manage to find something to eat: sample food or such things. I am quite resourceful. Sometimes I help myself in supermarkets, too.

When Myer's closes for the day, off I go to find somewhere else. The Southern Cross Hotel is a good spot. They have hot water in the toilets so I can wash. Most of the time, though, I spend at the Queen Victoria Hospital, in the toilets or sitting in the waiting room. There are always girls waiting for appointments so I pretend that is what I am doing and nobody seems to notice. I am not going to let the authorities know that I have nowhere to go, because then they've got me. I am not going back into an institution. I am on my own now.

Graeme keeps in touch when he feels like it, but I'm not really sure what he wants from me. I don't know what I am going to do with the baby anymore. I suppose I will have to give it up for adoption. Graeme is probably right: no one will let an orphan raise a baby, especially on her own. But sometimes I think I would like to try. I don't know. What do I know about raising a child? Bloody Graeme. He could have stayed with me until the baby was born, at least, but no, he had to go.

I go to the hospital for a final check-up and the doctor tells me I am malnourished. I have to be admitted to hospital. At least I will have a bed to sleep in. After a few days I tell the nurses that I have pains in my stomach, so I can stay longer.

While I am there, I ask a nurse how big the scar on my belly will be after the baby is born.

You're not having a Caesarean, she says. You won't have a scar.

So I say, Well, how am I going to have the baby?

And the nurse says, We'd better get the social worker to come and have a talk to you.

So the social worker comes and she tells me that the baby is going to be born through my vagina.

No way, I think. That is not possible. They are punishing me now. I am not even in the orphanage, and they are still going to make me suffer by having this baby through the vagina when most people get to go to sleep and have it cut out.

So when my water breaks a week later I am terrified. I am on the street, and I start to panic because my baby is going to come and I don't understand about this thing coming out of such a little hole. I must be making quite a scene because a stranger offers to take me to the hospital.

In the labour ward I can hear a woman screaming in pain.

Don't worry, one of the nurses tells me, it's just a wog. They always scream and scream.

They shave my private parts, give me an enema, put my legs up in stirrups and now I am really freaking out. A red-headed nurse stands over me saying, You'll never do this again, will you?

No, no, no, I won't do this again. I am screaming in pain and the red-headed nurse is trying to shut me up. Only the wogs scream.

YOUTH WELFARE DIVISION BIRTH NOTICE

Child: male
Date of birth: 20.4.68
Place of birth: Melbourne
Placement: . . .

They take the baby away. I am told it is better not to see the child if I am giving him up for adoption. I don't know what to do. I don't want to give the baby up but how can I keep him? The social worker says it is a big job to raise a baby and, being an orphan, I won't have any family help. She says I should give him up. I ask the nurse how they are going to feed him and she tells me not to worry, that all the excess breast milk goes into a big vat to be given to babies like mine. I am given pills to dry up my own supply.

Graeme comes in to see me. He doesn't say much and I don't say much to him but he is nice about everything. He goes down to the nursery and holds the baby.

Then his mother comes in. She is a cold sort of woman. Suspicious. But she sees the baby and decides he looks like Graeme. This seems to be her proof that he really is the father.

So now she says she wants me to keep the baby after all, and that we should call him Wayne and she will do whatever she can to help me.

Yes, yes, yes, I tell her. I will keep the baby. This is like a lottery win for me.

So now I have the baby and, oh wow!, I can have him in my room. I do whatever the nurses say because I know nothing. The Welfare is notified and the social worker comes to see me. She helps me find a live-in job in North Fitzroy, where I can take the baby and where they will lend me a cot and a bassinette and a highchair.

Wayne stays in hospital while I settle in. The family is a lovely young New Zealand couple with two little girls. I help the wife, cleaning and caring for her children. There is a lot to do but I don't mind hard work. I earn ten dollars a week and then Graeme gives me six dollars a week child support.

A couple of weeks later I bring Wayne home from the hospital. Now I am really a mother. I feed the baby, swaddle him up, put him back to bed. Sterilise the bottles and boil the nappies. But then the baby starts to cry and I don't know how to quieten him down. I change him, clean him, put him back to bed, and still he cries. How do I quieten this poor baby? I never think to play with the baby, cuddle the baby. Back in the orphanage, the babies were just left in their cots. No one liked them, no one cared for them, kissed them, stroked them. I don't know how to like my own baby. Imagine getting to the age of nearly eighteen and never having been cared for like that. Never having had someone's arms around you, soothing you. Plus, it is a terrible stigma to be a single mother and an orphan at the same time. My prospects are not good. I know people look down on me. I can't put Wayne in a pram and walk down the street with my head held high.

Graeme comes over to help me sometimes. There is nothing

between us but he is much better at being a parent than I am. Picking Wayne up and comforting him. He knows how to be a father. Sometimes Graeme takes us to his mother's house for dinner, but I think his mother looks down on me. I can see her thinking, How low could her son have gone to have had a child to someone like me? I am conscious of my weak left hand, the one the doctor bandaged too tightly when I fell off the swing at the orphanage. My wish has come true. *Please God deform me in any way but don't let me wet the bed.* Now I hide my hand, another secret to keep. I know Graeme's mother has spotted it and is looking at it with disgust.

Mostly Graeme just takes Wayne to see his mother on his own. I am not really welcome.

15th August, 1968

Miss L.E. Davis,
116 Queens Parade,
NORTH FITZROY.

Dear Lois,

As your term of control by this Branch expired on 15.7.68, it is necessary to make arrangements to hand over the savings which have accrued to you during the period you were with us . . .

Yours faithfully,

B.A. KEDDIE.
DIRECTOR OF YOUTH WELFARE

Now that I have turned eighteen I am officially on my own. No longer a ward of the state. That must mean I am almost a normal person now.

I stay at my job for about a year but then the family suddenly goes back to New Zealand and I find myself on the street again, only this time with a baby.

I really need help now. I simply don't know what to do with this baby. I am desperate for someone just to take my hand and guide me: this is what you do, this is how you feel. Or someone just to give me affection.

Wayne and I head back to Heidelberg and Graeme's mother. She lives in an empty old corner-block house, and I knock on her door and tell her I haven't got anywhere to live. Maybe she can help me like she promised. Her children have left home and she has spare rooms.

But she says she has changed her mind. She can't help me, doesn't want anything to do with me anymore, I will have to go. Her voice is so cold, it is as though I am a stranger off the street, a door-to-door saleswoman whose wares she doesn't need.

I had assumed she would take me in. Now I am standing on her doorstep with my bags and my baby – her grandson – and she shuts the door in my face.

I turn around and walk up the still street with the babe and nowhere to go.

CHAPTER 9

Jane from the orphanage, plus another girl and I decide to get a house together in inner-city Kew. The rent is twenty dollars a week, which Jane and I manage by getting jobs waitressing at the Southern Cross Hotel, the fancy hotel in the city where I used to go to wash when I was pregnant. Each day I feed the baby, put him to sleep in his cot with a bottle or two and then hitchhike the 6 kilometres to work. Wayne is a toddler now but I never have the money for a sitter so I just have to leave him there on his own. Stick some toys in his cot to keep him entertained, a wooden spoon and some pots and pans. He has a few proper little toys – things Graeme has given him or ones I have taken from the waiting room at the doctor's.

I work eight-hour shifts most days and when I am not working days I am working nights. It is hard. I accumulate my breaks from work and instead of taking lunch or morning tea, I sneak out and hitchhike back to the house to feed and change the baby. Put a fresh bottle and a new lot of toys in the cot. Then back to work. Sometimes I do it two or three times a day. I seem always to be on the road, rushing and tired. Jane covers for me, if needs be.

This poor baby, left alone day in and day out. Sometimes I get home to a terrible mess. The baby has filled his nappy and ripped it off. There is shit everywhere, all over his face, his mouth. I am not a very good mother.

Jane tells me that since I am only eighteen I need to have some fun, and so she sets me up on a blind date with a friend of her boyfriend. I like Darryl straightaway. He is tall and ruggedly handsome with dark, curly hair. A real gentleman, calm and kind.

Darryl is a builder. He takes me for drives through Melbourne, past his favourite heritage houses, and tells me how his dream is to buy a beautiful old terrace in East Melbourne and do it up. Once we are officially going out together, he introduces me to his friends and they become my friends. Nobody knows about my past – I tell them my family lives in the country – and I feel like an equal. We all go out and have a ball. These people are so privileged, they don't have a care in the world. Sometimes we leave Wayne with Darryl's mum and go to the beach or waterskiing down the Murray. Darryl is always an observer because he is scared of the water. He can't swim. And then we end up at the Burvale Hotel or Darryl's mum's house in Box Hill. Everyone calls her P – her real name is Olive – and she is wonderful. I take Wayne to see her as much as possible and she treats me like I am her own daughter. She doesn't know about my background but I do tell her I have no family, so she gives me my first taste of family life. We spend Christmas at her house and it is better than I could ever imagine. Wayne and I receive presents from everyone and Darryl tells us that his family is our family.

I start to learn that this is the way you treat someone you care about. Darryl loves Wayne and me, and with time I realise that he is my first love. Sometimes it scares me. I have never known this closeness before. It is strange having this man loving me. There are moments when I can't stand it. I can't stand him coming near me. He wants to cuddle me and kiss me. Make love and other things I never knew you did. I can't believe you do this sort of stuff. And he expects the same! You can't do that.

I fight it because I simply do not understand this closeness. He puts his arms around me and I want to break away: What do you want? What do you want from me? In nineteen years no one has touched me like that.

Even then, Darryl is good about it. He never pushes me.

It is like I have two lives: my life with Darryl and his family, and my life in Kew with Jane, waitressing and looking after Wayne and struggling to pay the bills. We can barely manage the basics when the going is good, but then one day the girl Jane and I live with takes off with the rent money. Disappears, never to be seen again. So not only are we a month behind on the rent, but now there are only two of us to cover the twenty dollars a week and the bills. Neither of us knows how to manage money as it is, so now I have to work double shifts.

I am on the road hitchhiking the whole time. From Kew to the city and back again. Sometimes I take taxis and do a runner, jumping out halfway and bolting. It is a nightmare. Finally, we can't keep up the rent on the place.

Jane finds herself another apartment while Darryl helps me find a live-in job with a lovely family close to his mother's house in Box Hill. Already I am more experienced at looking after children, and now I can be with Wayne all the time while I work for the family's two kids. Sometimes their mother even watches Wayne for me when I have time off. She is very sweet, although I cannot believe the decadence of her shopping. She buys every type of cereal that there is: Weet-Bix, Corn Flakes, Rice Bubbles, Coco Pops. Everything. The bottom floor of her pantry is like a supermarket. It strikes me that these kids have whatever they want; they are so free, they make their own choices. I start to realise I have never had choices. But this is not the orphanage anymore. This is family. It is so different to what I am used to. The mother loves her children. I watch and copy her, learning to give Wayne affection.

Anyway, now I am closer to Darryl and his mum, and more than ever it feels like I am a part of their family. I pretend P is my own mother and her other kids say that it is okay with them. It has taken my whole life but finally I have found a place where I belong.

Graeme still comes around, too, helping with Wayne and taking him to visit his mother. But things start to change after the move to Box Hill. For some reason, Graeme decides that if you have a baby you can't have a boyfriend. He doesn't like me seeing Darryl. He says it means I am a slut and am just like my mother.

He tells me I am a bad mother, which is true – and he doesn't even know that I used to leave Wayne alone when I worked at the Southern Cross.

Then one day, late in 1970 when Wayne is about two and a half, Graeme turns up and tells me that he is going to take me to court for custody of Wayne. He says for sure I won't win; he is going to find ways to prove what a bad mother I am and the judge will never leave a baby with an orphan who has no family support. He says his lawyer told him all this, so it is true.

There is no way I can go to court. I have no money. Who would represent me? I do not want to get tied up with authority again. And I am just so tired. I am only twenty. I don't know how I have managed to raise Wayne for this long. So I succumb to Graeme.

I may as well give him to you now, I say. Why don't you take him?

All right, I will, he says.

So Graeme gets the legal papers while I set about packing up Wayne's few little bits and pieces. Bottles and bibs and doctor-surgery toys. Then Graeme takes me to Heidelberg police station where I sign away my rights to my little boy. I feel awful about doing this to Wayne.

Graeme says, You've got thirty days to change your mind. But after he takes the baby and I don't have to wake up in the middle of the night anymore, and I don't have to have a live-in job, I just feel relieved.

Even so, I think of that poor child constantly. My mother left me and now I am leaving my own baby. I think I can only go through with it because always, deep in my heart, I cling to the feeling that one day I will get him back.

A couple of days after I lose Wayne, Darryl turns up to take me out. He asks where Wayne is.

I gave him to his father, I say.

What do you mean?

I adopted him out. His father has him now.

What, just like that? Without telling me, you just did that? You didn't think to speak to me first?

No. Graeme said he would take me to court and get him anyway, so I said he could have him now.

Darryl looks at me very strangely. He can't understand. He thinks I am the weirdest person for doing this. But Darryl doesn't know about my life.

So instead of trying to explain myself, I say to him, I'm going away now.

What do you mean? Darryl asks.

I'm free.

CHAPTER 10

Twenty years old, I stand on the side of the road with my bags at my feet and stick my thumb out. I haven't got a clue where I am going. For the first time in my life I can go anywhere and no one will come after me. Not the government, not Graeme and his mother. Nobody. I am on my own.

An old white Mercedes pulls over and the man behind the wheel asks where I am headed.

Wherever you are, I say.

Well, I'm going to Sydney, he says.

Then I'm going to Sydney.

All right, hop in.

His name is Hermann; he's an older man, maybe forty. A solid Eastern European. He buys me dinner on the way and, when we reach Sydney, offers me a bed at his place. No strings attached. He doesn't even want sex, he says. He just enjoys my company. I accept and he drives me to his house in Fitzwilliam Road, Vaucluse. One of the best streets in one of the best areas of Sydney, he tells me. How lucky am I?

Hermann lives with another man above a rundown timber shop. But the road is wide, with trees and beautiful, large houses overlooking the water. There is another girl staying here too. Her name is Jayne and she and I become permanent fixtures in Fitzwilliam Road. I don't know what is in it for Hermann except that he seems to enjoy taking care of us. Maybe he just likes having girls around.

I love Sydney. I have no baby and no one knows anything about me, I can be anyone I want; just like everybody else. I get a job as a receptionist in a real estate agency and Jayne teaches me about boys and how to do my hair; tease it up, curl it, put a hairpiece in my ponytail. She shows me how to dress and I splurge on a fabulous pair of bottle green, velvet bell-bottoms with a matching jacket and tie. Every Wednesday night, Jayne and I dress up and go down to the Royal Oak Hotel in Double Bay, because that is where all the single guys go. People tell me how pretty I am and boys start liking me. I feel good about myself.

When I tell people I am from Melbourne, they say, Well, you're lucky then because you have landed in the best area of Sydney. I definitely don't tell anyone about my real past. I am from Melbourne, I have family who live in the country and I am an only child. End of story.

One night at the Oak I meet this very suave, very handsome, blond guy called Greg Sinclair, and he becomes my two-day-a-week boyfriend. Every Wednesday and Saturday night, Greg and I go out. He probably has a Tuesday and Thursday girl too, who knows? It suits me fine to have some fun without complications because I can't get Darryl out of my thoughts. Even though love is still a very difficult concept for me, I am confronted with the reality of how much he means to me. It wasn't him I was leaving when I escaped Melbourne, it was all the emotions that I couldn't deal with. So we still speak on the phone and visit each other when we can. There is a sense of commitment even though he has other girlfriends down in Melbourne and I have Greg.

Greg has a real estate business and lots of money. His family has a beautiful mansion by the water at Parsley Bay and Greg lives in the bungalow out the back. He takes me to the best restaurants and we drink champagne, and when I stay overnight with him he sends me to work the next day in a chauffeur-driven Rolls-Royce. People always stare when I'm dropped off.

We go on like this for several months until one day he says, I'm going to Hong Kong now, so I won't be seeing you.

Rightio, I say, see you later.

(Years down the track, in 1978, I watch Greg on the telly as he visits his father, William Sinclair, in a Thai jail where he has been convicted of heroin trafficking.)

I move out of Fitzwilliam Road and into a big place in the northern beaches suburb of Manly with a friend of Darryl's called Jimmy Coghan. Darryl has asked him to watch out for me because Darryl is going on a Pacific cruise for a few weeks over Christmas and he wants to make sure I am okay.

Shortly before he is due to leave on his cruise, Darryl phones. As the conversation stumbles along I realise he has something he wants to tell me. He is talking about how important I am to him; how he values the closeness we have and how he thinks of us as a unit. Darryl is more rogue than romantic, so it is an awkward conversation, made all the more so because I find it extremely embarrassing to hear such things about myself. The idea that someone likes me, that they want me, makes my cheeks burn. While I feel the same way about him, I am even more hopeless at expressing my feelings than he is. But somehow we muddle through these messy declarations of love and it becomes clear that, above all, we just want to be together.

And that's when Darryl says, When I get back from the cruise, you and I will get hitched.

It is no bended-knee declaration, but it is a proposal, Darryl-style. And to me that is a promise of a good life. I know that with Darryl there is love, comfort, laughs and a sense of security.

More than that, though, marriage means family. It means children. And in the back of my mind, I have the idea that marrying Darryl might be my opportunity to get Wayne back.

It is December 1971. Darryl rings to say goodbye before heading off on his cruise. He says his ship is going to dock in Sydney on Saturday evening for an overnight stay and asks me if I will meet him.

I tell him of course I will, and we make arrangements for Jimmy and me to meet him at the docks at 9 p.m.

Saturday rolls around and I can't wait for it to be night-time so I can see Darryl. P calls during the day, saying she needs to talk to Jimmy. I tell her he is not around but she wants me to find him and call her back. I haven't managed to track him down when the phone rings again.

Darryl's sister, Dana, wants me to find Jimmy, too. She says she needs to talk to us together, but I tell her I don't have time to go out looking for Jimmy because I am supposed to be getting ready to meet Darryl at the docks for dinner. Jimmy is meant to be coming with me, I tell her.

Yeah, he'll bring you, she says.

All right.

So I continue getting ready, and Jimmy still hasn't turned up when the phone rings again and it is Darryl's best mate, Kevin. Can you find Jimmy? he asks me.

Finally I think, Why on earth does everybody want me to find Jimmy? Darryl is not coming till 9 p.m.; I'll be fine. I will get down to the docks on my own if I have to.

P phones back. You can't get hold of Jimmy?

No, I don't know where he is. Someone said he's at the pub. The Steyne pub or whatever it is, at Manly. But I'm not going down there; I don't know where he is and I would rather be at the boat at nine o'clock.

I am standing by the window, looking out across the water, and P says, Lois, you have to sit down. I want to talk to you.

All right, what is going on?

You won't be going to the docks at nine o'clock.

What? That bastard is not going to marry me now, is that it?

I say to P, So it looks like I'm not getting married then.

No, it's nothing to do with that.

What then?

I really would prefer to tell you this when you're with Jimmy.

Well, I don't know where he is.

Lois, Darryl won't be coming to Sydney this evening. Something terrible happened last night.

What?

Darryl fell overboard and they think he's dead.

Bloody hell, what are you talking about? He's dead? Where is he?

They can't find his body.

Nuh. He's pulling a trick. There is no way. Darryl can't swim. He's scared of the water. Darryl can't swim!

Then Darryl's sister phones me. It's true, she says. My husband is on his way to collect you.

Nuh. No way.

Something inside me snaps. I put down the phone and run out into the street, but I don't know who to go to or what to do. I just don't know. I am so alone. I am crying like never before. My first real emotion. It aches inside. I just can't stop crying, screaming. Why has he left me like this? Why? He loved me and now he is gone. I run through the streets until I find Jimmy in the pub and I'm kicking him and whacking him. It's like an explosion. I am going mad. I'm mental. Oh my God I want Darryl. Poor Darryl. We have too much for him to be dead. He is only twenty-three.

P arranges for me to return to Melbourne. I move into her house and she puts me in Darryl's room. I don't know how to feel. My life has not equipped me to handle this. It is just so horrible.

All we can do is sit and wait for Darryl's body to be found. Apparently, he'd had a few drinks – Darryl liked to drink. Beer. Bacardi and Coke. He was laughing, excited. It was his first time on a boat and he was going on holidays. Maybe he was thinking, Well, I'm going away for a good time and then I'll come back and marry Lois.

He lost his balance. One fellow went in after him, trying to save him. Everyone was looking but they just couldn't find him. It was dark and the water was murky.

The ship hadn't even left Melbourne, it was still at the dock.

He fell overboard. Those words keep playing in my head, I can't help it. *He fell overboard. He fell overboard.* Bloody idiot.

It is on Christmas Eve, a week later, that we watch on the television news as the police drag Darryl's body, like a sack of potatoes, from the water onto a boat. It is so bad. I feel sorry for P.

Darryl's brother has to go and identify his body. I want to go and see him but I am not allowed. Apparently, he is quite bloated and P says it would upset me.

Then there is the funeral in Doncaster, which is awful. I am so sad after this. I miss Darryl very much. It is too hard to let him go. P says, I have lost my son but I have a daughter now. I spend time with his younger brother, John, because he looks so much like Darryl. Younger, and a bit of a hippie, but otherwise the spitting image. I want to close my eyes and kiss him. We are standing close, our bodies touching. I am kissing him, wanting him to be Darryl. But he pushes me away. I want to make love with Darryl through him and he won't let me. I wish he would.

One night, lying in Darryl's bed, I wake up and Darryl is there, standing at the edge of the bed. He is standing over me, vivid as can be. And I am saying, Oh my God, why? Come to me. Come to me.

But the moment I register, he is gone. I desperately want to close my eyes and get him back again. Come back, come back, come back.

I have a photo of Darryl blown up to the size of a poster and hang it above my bed.

Darryl's mates decide they are going to take care of me. They ring me up to check on me, come around every once in a while to help me out. And P is my mum now. She cooks for me and takes care of me. Every now and then I find twenty dollars in my purse. She just slips it in there for me. Sometimes we sit and chat, P in her rocking chair and me next to her. We go to auctions together and she bids on old bits and pieces. She is a collector of rubbish, I suppose. Nothing of value. She is a lovely lady. I am really lucky.

All this love and attention makes me decide I want to see more of my own family. I am not really in touch with Scarlet any longer; she thinks I am too much like our mother, because I had a child and gave him up. And I haven't seen much of Tommy since that awful time in Sydney. We just don't have the skills to stay in touch. I do have a relationship with June, though. We get on well and she lives near me in Melbourne so we see a lot of each other. I have a sense of family with June.

One day, June comes to see me to tell me she has an address for our father. She says he is living in the bush, at a place called Tooma, near Albury on the New South Wales–Victoria border.

She says she is going to go and see him and leaves me the directions in case I decide to go too.

I guess I will go and meet Bill Davis.

I ask a friend if he will drive me to Albury so I can spend the Easter break with my dad. I don't tell him that I have never met my dad. I just say that he has moved since I last saw him so I am not entirely sure where we are going. The whole six-hour drive I keep thinking to myself, How do I pretend I know my father when we get there? How can I recognise him so I don't blow my cover? And I keep saying to my friend, You know you won't be able to stay. You're not invited.

In Tooma, we stop and ask for directions to the Davis house and are pointed along a dusty, potholed road. I can see a tall old man in the distance. You can tell he would have been handsome in his day. He has a chicken in his hand and kids running all around him. I know straightaway he is my father.

Quick, stop the car, I tell my friend. There is no way I am going to have him meet my father the complete stranger. You'd better go, I say. Come back in five days. Quick, go go go go go. I am getting upset with him now. Just go.

My friend must think it is all a bit weird but he drives off, and I am left standing there with my suitcase.

My father walks up to me and says, You're Lois, aren't you?

Yes.

Strange how we know each other. And immediately it feels right. At last I have a father. Maybe I can even call him Dad. What do I say to this complete stranger?

The kids come running up to us, more coming from inside the house. There are five of them, and June is here too.

Who are these children? I ask my father.

They're mine, he says.

Oh.

I didn't know he had children. A whole new family. No one told me that.

The kids start encircling me – my new brothers and sisters – and they are all welcoming me and shepherding me into the house. I am one of the family. In the kitchen I am introduced to a very thin, dark-haired woman called Jean, who is my dad's wife, and then to each of the five children: Warren, Cheryl, Gary, Jimmy and Betty. Warren and Cheryl are close to my age and pretty little Betty, the youngest, is about three. It is crowded and chaotic in their tiny shack, with my dad chopping the head off the chook, which continues to flop around after it is dead, and Jean plucking it for our dinner. The kids are helping too, in between chattering to me. I feel strange in the middle of it all. It is a bit bar-baric to me. They are so poor, they have nothing. Their clothes are from the Salvation Army and the kitchen is a mess and they all sleep together. Jean's hands are bony and calloused and she works like a slave. Yet these kids have a mum and a dad, they have each other. They have a real life, and it looks so good. I just want to claim them as my own. My family. And they are doing everything they can to make me feel welcome. They keep saying, I'm your sister. Or, I'm your brother. They want to accept me. And I like that there are no airs and graces, even though I am being a bit of a princess. Can I dare to think that I am? They actually think that I'm posh. No one has ever thought that of me before.

And there is my father. We look at each other and I say, So you're my dad?

Yeah, I'm your dad.

My dad.

After dinner, my dad says, Why don't we go down the pub for a quiet drink so we can have a proper talk. Just you and me. It's too noisy here.

I have been wanting this so bad, to be alone with my dad, just him and me without all these other kids around. So I do my hair and put on a bit of lippy because I want my dad to be proud of me, and we get in his beaten-up Holden and drive to the pub in Tooma for a beer and a chat. He tells me how he was actually the one who came looking for us. He found June the first day he started searching. That is how easy it was. The day he went looking for us, he found us. Now June has basically moved in permanently and here I am, too.

He tells me how he lost the farm that he had in Gippsland where we were all born because my mother emptied out the bank account, forging his signature on cheques. Then he met Jean in Melbourne, and after they had a couple of kids they moved out to western New South Wales. Dad worked as a rabbit trapper and they travelled around a lot, living in tents on different properties. They came to the Murray River about ten years ago.

We finish our drinks and leave the pub to drive the lonely road home. Before we get there, my father stops the car in the middle of nowhere. It is pitch black outside and I can smell the beer and smoke on my father's breath. He moves towards me and puts his arms around me.

I want to give my daughter a kiss, he says.

In the darkness he pulls me towards him and tries to start kissing me. But this is not the way a father kisses his daughter. How can he be doing this to me? I am hit with panic. And then the smell. I can't stand the smell. Not the booze but the smell of a man going out to work all day. It is all over him, and my father is still grabbing at me and now I am yelling. Stop it. Get your hands off me. Get off. Take me back to the house right now.

He does. He just drives back to the house and I get out of the car and go to bed.

It is never mentioned after that but I can't look at his face.

That face that saw me as more than a daughter. And I never call him Dad again, either. I don't call him anything.

I feel like screaming: How could you do this to me, you idiot? I just wanted to be alone with my dad. I should have taken June with me, but no, I had to be alone with him.

Now the sight of my father makes me sick but it is not enough for me to turn away completely. I stay out my visit and I keep in contact once I am gone. What did he think, that I was going to get this close and then let him snatch it all away? All in a matter of hours? No way. I am part of this family now and he is not going to destroy that for me.

Even though I still see my father, we never really speak again; there is an awkwardness between us and I give him a hard time. Something inside me likes to torment him. How dare he leave us kids, and go and have another family as though we didn't exist.

He still tries desperately to talk to me. He wants to tell me about the family. Every time he starts up, I cut him off. I say, I am talking to Warren, I'm not talking to you. It is all front. Inside I am dying to find out more about my family.

I do like the children very much, though. They are so happy-go-lucky. Especially Warren. We click and spend a lot of time together. He comes to the city and I show him around, still with hayseed in his hair and me in my miniskirts and foot-high hairdo. Warren teaches me to drive. I probably have a closer relationship with these kids than I do with Scarlet, June and Tommy. (I never meet my other sister Mary, who remains institutionalised.) It is probably because they were brought up properly.

At least now I am not an orphan. I have family. I don't have to tell fantasy stories anymore.

I meet my mother again, too. Living with some man, still in the boarding house in St Kilda. Still dragging on a Camel cigarette.

She never looks up at me, except to sneak a glance and ask, Where is Scarlet?

Don't you know who I am? I say. It's me, Lois. Don't you remember me? Look at me.

I am getting cross. I want her to want me. To acknowledge me, at least. Feel something for me, for Christ's sake, woman! At one point I even want to say 'Mum', but I can't get the word out.

What do I call this woman? She is still quite disgusting, sitting in this room talking bullshit with her cigarette hanging out of her mouth. Do I really want to get to know this person who claims to be my mother? She has an awful smell. I can't stand it. It is Mary Fishpot all over again. I have to get out of here. I check that there is an open door where I can make a quick escape. I want a mother to be proud of, not Dorothy Davis. Couldn't God have dished me out someone better?

Where is Scarlet? she keeps asking.

It is not that she doesn't want to know about me. She is just not capable of connecting with me.

The first thing I decide to do after leaving my mother that day is to change my name. Only a mother who has raised you has the right to name you. Besides, I really don't like the name Lois. Lois is that scungy girl from the orphanage who people don't like. She is Mary Fishpot. She is the girl all Darryl's friends nicknamed Low-arse. Here comes Low-arse. They never realised how they were hurting me. But mostly it's that the name Lois relates to my mother.

I remember back to being in the orphanage when I was in about grade three and three sisters arrived. Normally, you had to be three years old to go to St Aidan's, but Donna was allowed to come with her two big sisters even though she was only eighteen months. Everyone usually hated the babies but for some reason they loved Donna. She was carried around everywhere and cuddled and held hands with Norma, the girl who looked after the babies. We had never seen anyone get this kind of attention. The kid was queen of the whole orphanage.

So I name myself after that little baby who got all the cuddles. Goodbye, Lois. I am Donna Davis now.

CHAPTER 11

I eventually move out of P's and rent a little bachelor apartment near Jane in the posh suburb of Toorak. I don't want to go back to Sydney and leave P – she is trying to help me and I am trying to help her – but it is time to get back out on my own.

Jane and I take jobs as hostesses at an upmarket club called the Top Hat in Bourke Street. Politicians and businessmen drink there. Super-rich men, high society men who you read about in the paper. Jane and I have to sit and drink with them, and the more drinks they have, the more money we earn. So I order champagne, which is really lolly water, and pour it on the carpet.

I am not interested in men at all. I still have the enlarged photo of Darryl hanging above my bed. But some of the men from the Top Hat take a fancy to me. There is a very wealthy dairy farmer, called John, who always wants to sit with me. He is probably about forty, and a lovely man, but old in my eyes. I am only twenty-one. He starts offering me things. He has a house in Lansell Road, Toorak and he wants to marry me and give me a first-class plane ticket around the world. Big deal.

It all means nothing to me. I realise that if I take all of that I will have to have sex with him. And I am not going to. It is a bit like the German couple who wanted to adopt me back at the orphanage. They were offering me all this stuff but I would have to live with them and be in their family. Not on your life.

There is another Top Hat regular called Gordon. He is some business bigwig. He is even older – grey hair, maybe fifty – but I click a bit better with him. He is slightly rougher, more like Darryl, whereas John seems more of a blue blood and he bores me with his money talk.

Sometimes I see Gordon away from the Top Hat. He drives a beautiful big blue Mercedes and one night he is too drunk to go home so he comes back to my house. We end up in bed and I am thinking, Oh dear, I am obligated here. We hug and he tries to kiss me but I am repulsed. I tell him, No, I can't do this.

I physically cannot bring myself to do anything. In my eyes, these men are more like my father. I am not going to have sex with my father.

Gordon is fine with it, luckily.

Not long after that, I am at home by myself one day when a Myer's delivery truck pulls up outside my apartment. The driver opens the back of the truck and tells me I can have whatever I want. I can't believe it. It is filled with furniture, paintings, whitegoods – anything I could possibly need. Which is a lot, because all I have in my apartment is a mattress on the floor.

I phone Gordon and say, There's a Myer's truck at my house. Do you know anything about this?

He says, Take whatever you want. You need some furniture in that place. I really want you to do it. I will be insulted if you don't.

I say, I don't have to have sex, do I?

No, don't be silly.

So I get this slick little stereo, and I've never had a stereo before in my life, and a television. Now I have linen and blankets. A fridge. Gordon doesn't know it but in some ways he is my surrogate father. I have P as my mother and now I have found myself a father.

After a while, Gordon asks me to move in with him. He says that we will get a big house in Toorak and I start to warm to the idea. Yeah, I say, and I'll cook you dinner every night, and I'll do this and I'll do that. But he says, I don't want a girl to do that, I just want a girl to go out with. He wants me to be this consort who drives around in a lovely car and has nice nails. To be more like his mistress, I suppose. He doesn't want a domestic situation because he has just come through a divorce. He already has a family.

Oh, no then, I say. I know I could never fit into the society he moves in.

That all comes to an end, because the Top Hat folds and I move on to a job as a receptionist at an advertising agency in Fitzroy. I don't have the right experience – I have only ever done waitressing, really, and a brief stint answering phones at the real estate agency in Sydney – but I get the job because I am pretty, I think.

Nevertheless, I have it in my head that I am going places. I have a nice little flat in a fancy suburb and I am going to work hard and make some money for myself. I won't just marry a man and take his money. I will make the money. One day I will even buy myself a house. The one thing I have learnt is how to work.

This determination to be self-sufficient is a driving force within me. It must stem from having had the Welfare take care of me for most of my life. I am not going to let that happen again. The way I see it, the only way I can own my life is if I support myself.

So I start on the reception desk at Film House, which is Fred Schepisi's production company. (This is a few years before he makes his name by writing and directing *The Devil's Playground*, so he is still making television commercials.) I have trouble

97

pronouncing 'Schepisi' and it drives him mad. Some of his first instructions to me are, You have to spell my name correctly and pronounce it properly. Which is fair enough.

Most days, Fred and the others go out for long, long lunches and return to work the worse for wear. Then I have to listen to Fred's stories about his boarding school and how bad it was. I don't drink much so I feel a little out of place. I basically keep to myself, as I never really feel good enough in other people's company, but I do my job well. I must say, I like Fred. He is an original and a good bloke.

After a while, I am moved into production and casting, which means I actually get to work on the ads. I feel like I am at the pinnacle. We are casting for a jeans commercial and it is my job to find a great bum. All these girls come in, try on the jeans, turn around – but none fit the brief. Then everyone starts saying to me, You have a great bum. So I say, Okay, give me the jeans.

Yeah, yeah. You've got it. You've got the bum.

So I cast myself and do the shoot. When I get the pay cheque, I think, Wow, this is better than working in an office every day. Plus, when I listen to the other models talking about their travels to Asia and Europe, I start dreaming of getting away. I have never been out of the country. Everyone keeps saying how pretty I am, so I go to see an agent at Vivien's modelling agency. She says, Just get your portfolio together, you'll be right.

And I go on the books at Vivien's.

I am going to castings, looking good, getting enough work to make a living. I model with some of the English girls who come over to work in Australia, and with Belinda Green, who is about to become Miss World. I do a shoot with the famous photographer Helmut Newton for a Qantas commercial –

another bum job, lying naked amongst some rocks – and he takes some great shots of me, topless with my hair in a bob. I am photographed by the legendary Bruno Benini and Patrick Russell, who do a lot of work for *Vogue*. Soon I have enough money to buy myself a car – a white Torana XU1 like Peter Brock's car – and I am paying it off myself. Life is great.

I start hanging out with a girl called Carmel, who introduces me to marijuana and Leonard Cohen, Cat Stevens and Bob Dylan records. We get stoned and laugh a lot.

Carmel is far more worldly than me; very clever and politically-minded. She is going to move to Israel and live in a kibbutz one day. She has a bit of a big nose but she is much classier than me. I am kind of gangly and dumb, just a pretty face. She gets all the boyfriends, too, because she will go to bed with them and I won't.

Carmel and I are driving down St Kilda Road towards the modelling agency one day, when we spot a good-looking guy overtaking us in a Mini Moke.

Come on, Carmel says to me, let's chase him.

So I speed up the Torana, with Carmel geeing me up: Pull up alongside him! Come on, quick!

The traffic lights ahead turn red and we pull to a stop beside his car. I sneak a better look and he is incredibly handsome. Wavy shoulder-length blond hair and blue eyes. I am instantly attracted to this hippie.

Carmel winds down the window and yells out to him, Do you wanna come with us?

Yeah, okay.

Follow us!

So he follows us back to Carmel's place in East St Kilda, where Carmel rolls a joint and lights up. Our dream man introduces himself as Robert Ehrenburg. He is an actor and a model too. Eighteen months older than me.

I become very withdrawn and quiet. I have never gone after a man. I don't know what to do. Anyway, it looks like Carmel will be having him. I sit with them, while Carmel does all the talking and I do nothing, until it starts to get dark outside and I am feeling flat.

Oh well, I guess I'd better go home, I say, resigned to leaving Robert there with Carmel. But then he says, Oh yeah, I've got to go too.

He comes running down after me and says, Do you want to go out with me tomorrow?

So I say to him, You can come over, if you like.

Robert arrives at my house with a punnet of strawberries. Sexy in a pair of jeans, he is funny and silly, and we fall for each other instantly.

He invites me down to Phillip Island for the weekend.

All right, okay.

So we drive down and we are lying there on the beach, and he is stroking my hair, saying, You've got such beautiful hair.

Nobody has ever done this and said these kinds of things to me before. Darryl wasn't like this. He was more like me. Detached. Robert is more European in the way he acts. He is Dutch, so he is always saying things like, You're so beautiful, your skin is so soft. I love you.

I'm thinking, Mmm, this feels nice.

Then I realise, He's getting too close. This means he is definitely going to want to do it with me. I can't. I can't do it. So I tell him, Actually, I might go home if that's okay. I don't really want to stay the night down here.

That's okay, he says. We'll go back. I'll drop you back at your place if you like.

Yes, please.

We drive all the way back to Melbourne in the middle of the night, me feeling nervous the whole way. He drops me home, and on his way out the door he kisses me on the lips ever so gently and asks, Can I come and see you tomorrow? He is unbelievably handsome.

Yeah, I say, we can hang out, if you like. That'd be nice.

It is the beginning of our love affair. The next day Robert moves in and after that we never leave each other's side. He teaches me how to love in a non-sexual way. He is such an interesting person. But also, we are insanely attracted to each other, we make love morning, noon and night. It is like nothing I have ever experienced; everything with him feels natural. I am madly in love.

Eventually, Robert looks at Darryl's picture above the bed and says, It's gotta go. You're not going to have that picture above the bed anymore.

So the picture goes and I must be ready to let Darryl go, too, because it feels okay. I even take Robert to meet P.

No matter how close we become, though, I do not tell Robert about my background: my orphanage upbringing and how I gave up my little boy. I am too ashamed. How could he love someone like that? As far as he is concerned, I have a family in the bush that I don't want to talk about because I don't get along with them. That usually stops any further discussion. And if not, I am very good at deflecting questions. I just change the subject to something he is interested in and he never even realises what I am doing.

It gets harder when Robert introduces me to his parents. His mother, Muffy, is determined to find out about my family. She has a need to know where I come from: And what does your mother do? And what does your father do? And where did you go to school? I am forever trying to change the subject but it keeps getting harder.

Muffy must sense I am hiding something, because I don't think she likes me much. I am not good enough for her son. She is a bit of a snob, and decides that if her son is going to persist in going out with me, I need to learn about the finer things in life. She is an antique dealer and has a great eye, so she teaches me about antiques and how to determine different types of wood. She gives me lessons on setting the table, manners, elocution – never cross your legs, don't move, speak clearly and look people in the eyes. And you must always wear lipstick, dear. You must never go out without it. It is like she is helping me to be reborn; I am coming out into the world properly. Robert helps in his own way, too. Each morning he decides what I should wear, and while I am in the shower he lays my clothes out on the bed. If I want to wear something else, he gets upset – it is important that I look a certain way – so I go along with his selection.

Robert's father is more accepting of me. His name is Jacobus but everyone calls him Ko and he is a mathematician at the university. He likes just to sit and read, smoke his cigars, often with a finger in his ear so as to block out Muffy and her nonsense. Yes, dear, he says every now and then.

While Muffy is busy reshaping me, she never lets up on finding out about my family and it starts to weigh on me. I feel like I have to tell Robert the truth. I don't like telling lies; it makes me anxious. But if I do tell the truth, he will leave me for sure – because if you grow up in an orphanage, you are the lowest of the low. Every day I am with him there are moments when I think, I have to tell him. But how?

We have been together six months when we are at a Wool Board function one night – a big do that all the models go to – and I drink too much champagne and blurt it out: I was an orphan. And then I tell him how I have a child and ask if he will help me to get him back.

Robert is in complete shock. He is angry. We have to leave

immediately. He says I lied to him. I should have told him this from the beginning. On and on. I can't believe what I have done. I have lost him now.

I go home but Robert decides he is not coming with me. He can't deal with this. He goes to his mother's or somewhere – he tells her I am an orphan. And Muffy's response, of course, is, Well, we can't have an orphan in the family. You don't know where she comes from, who her family is.

Robert takes time to cool off before he starts coming around again. Then he wants to find out about my family. I don't want to tell him the truth about my parents so I just keep saying that I am an orphan. He asks if there is any way we can investigate my background. I know it is really his mother who wants to know all this.

Robert says he wants to break up but at the same time he still loves me. Eventually, we come to an understanding: I won't tell anyone else I was an orphan, and Robert will move back in.

It is not the same, though. All those Mary Fishpot feelings have come up again. Muffy makes me feel like the girl nobody wants to be friends with. And now that Robert knows about my past, I beg him to help me get Wayne back but he says he will leave me if I do. Now we are fighting and I am having trouble once again with closeness. So when a model girlfriend of mine, Maggie Gill, says she is going to work in Japan, I decide to go with her. There is no discussion with Robert – I just up and leave. That is what I do with men.

Maggie helps me arrange a passport and in August 1972 we fly to Tokyo together, Maggie – tall, beautiful and sophisticated (she used to go out with Cat Stevens) – and me, petite and naïve. We get a place together and have an absolute ball. There are lots of boys around, always taking us out and doing things for us. I don't have a boyfriend – I suppose Robert is still in my heart – but we have a brilliant time. Japan is so modern. They have machines in the wall where you can withdraw money rather than having to go into the bank.

I join an agency called Now Fashion and the work starts rolling in. In Australia I am just another model but the Japanese love me. I am skinny and short so I fit into their clothes, and I have a sense of humour. In Japan I am *the* girl, and the money is amazing.

I am not shy about my body so I get a lot of the work that other girls won't do. At one casting I go to, for pure wool jumpers, they ask to check our breasts. In the ad, when you put the jumper on, the side of your breast will be seen. No one will show their boobs but I just pull up my top. There you go. I have okay breasts so I get the job and it pays $1000 a day for a three-day shoot. Three thousand dollars. It is a huge sum of money to me.

I work constantly for three months. I do a shoot for Yves Saint Laurent glasses that pays well and my jobs take me all over Japan. It is the best way to be a tourist. We spend more money than I have ever had before and even then, when my visa expires, I have still saved $10,000. Nearly enough to buy a house or a block of land.

From Japan, I fly to England to continue my travels. I stay with my old flatmate from Manly, Darryl's mate Jimmy Coghan, who is working as a stockbroker in London and living in Sloane Square. We flirt a bit but nothing happens because secretly I miss Robert. We are still in touch and still friends, despite Muffy's best efforts. (When I phone from Japan and she answers, she tells me to stay away from her son, and never to call again.)

It takes just three weeks in England for me to realise that I can't stay away from Robert any longer. I abandon my plans and return home.

Only once I am settled in Melbourne do I phone Robert and tell him I am back in town.

Oh, he says, I'm leaving to go overseas in a week. I'm going travelling through Asia.

So I have one week to woo him back.

CHAPTER 12

Robert comes over that night and instantly it is back on. The love is still there and I can't get enough of him. With only one week before he goes, we spend every day and night together, always careful that Muffy doesn't find out. We don't have time for her interference.

By the week's end, he tells me how much he loves me and asks me to travel with him. We are 100 per cent back together, and so, still without Muffy's knowledge, I join Robert travelling through Asia. We even fly out separately to avoid arousing his family's suspicions.

Our first stop is Bali. We stay close to the beach in primitive *losmans* with cold water and it is so romantic. I love every minute. We take lazy walks on the beach and explore temples; Robert surfs and I discover Balinese culture. It is magic.

The Balinese people seem so happy and contented with their lives. To see them tend to their rice paddies is a meditation in itself. I can watch them for hours. And I am fascinated by the Hindu offerings of flowers and food in ceremonial baskets peppering the roadside each day. Within this gentle, spiritual environment, I feel myself blossoming day by day. There is no negative feeling from the family here; it is just Robert and me.

We are becoming so close and we are deeply in love. He says the first part of my body he fell in love with was my feet. He thinks they are beautiful and he kisses them constantly. Under my breath, I say, Thank you, Mother Carmela.

From Bali, we travel up to central Java on an overcrowded bus with squawking chooks and people of all descriptions. We head out of the city, past mosques and paddy fields and horse-drawn carriages to the famous black sand dunes and huge surf of Parangtritis beach. These waters are the home of the Queen of the South Seas and there is a centuries-old legend that anyone who wears the Queen's favourite colour – green – to the beach will be swallowed by the sea. Apparently, quite a few people have drowned or disappeared here. Robert and I notice that the dress I am wearing has a little bit of green in the pattern. He says it's all right, it's just a little, even though the local people say I should get changed. We swim in the rough seas, but with Robert by my side I feel completely safe. We make love in the ocean, the beautiful beach totally deserted and untouched. A perfect place to be in love.

Despite the green in my dress I am not lured to my death, but within the hour I am delirious, with a high temperature and uncontrollable stomach pains – suspected malaria. They say the Queen has a preference for young men, anyway.

Robert has to get me to Java; a twenty-minute walk back to the boat, then from the boat on a tinfoil bus to the Dutch hospital. I am in hospital for a couple of weeks. Robert begs them to fly me back to Australia for treatment, but they won't let me go. They say, She will die if you take her out of here. Robert mentions the story of the Queen of the South Seas and they just nod. So he dotes on me, never leaving my side. I think this is when he truly falls in love with me. He tells me he can't imagine his life without me; I suppose he thinks I might die. It is very intense, and very romantic to have someone taking such good care of me, and while I am lying there in my narrow metal bed, with a fever and attached to a drip, he puts a beautiful coral and gold ring on my finger, and asks me to marry him.

No doubt buoyed by my elation I make a full recovery, and from Java we head to Hong Kong, where we take some modelling jobs until we have enough money saved to move on to Thailand. In Thailand we stay with a friend of ours, Michael Toole. Michael is a famous epidemiologist who came to Thailand to provide medical treatment for refugees and remote villagers. He lives in Chiang Mai, in the north of the country, in a beautiful old-style stilt house built from raw timber. He shares it with Rosie Pitman, a nurse.

Robert has been a Buddhist for about four years so we spend much of our time visiting temples, with Robert teaching me all about Buddhism. The peaceful philosophy appeals to my hippie leanings. I like the idea of becoming a vegetarian and practising meditation. Our travels open my eyes to the idea that there is more out there than the uptight British tradition in which I was brought up. The Asian approach to life seems so calm compared with that of the West. I love the architecture, the vibrant clothing and beautiful women, the tropical humidity soaking up the sweet scents of tuberose and mango and cinnamon.

What really impresses me, though, is the love and affection the people pour out to their children. The kids are absolutely adored. People will just sit and stare in wonder at their children.

Wayne is still in my heart and so I renew my pleas to Robert to help me get him back once we return home. But Robert just says, No, one day we will have our own children.

Then, in about April 1974, when we have been in Thailand a

month, I discover that I am pregnant. I tell Robert that we are having a baby.

His response is, Okay, we can get Michael to do the abortion.

They are not the words I want to hear at all. In truth, though, I am half expecting this reaction from him, so I am not as shocked as I might be. He has very set ideas about the way he wants to do things, and he has it in his head that I must wait until I am twenty-eight to have a baby. So I have already prepared a response. I say to him, No, I'll tell you what we are going to do. I will have an abortion if that is what you decide you want – Michael can organise it and I will go into the hospital. But after the abortion, it will be over between us. Because if you really want me to abort a child, it means you don't love me. However, if you do decide you want the baby, then we have to get married. Because I can't continue travelling pregnant and unmarried. I don't want this baby to be born without a father.

He is just nodding along, so I continue: What I suggest is that you go away – to a temple or wherever, anywhere you want to go – and you don't contact me for two days. I will wait here, and when you come back, you tell me what you want me to do. But the consequences are that we will either get married or we will never see each other again. And I am not playing games here.

Okay, he says.

So off he goes and when he returns he says, I love you. Let's have the baby.

We arrive in Taipei, Taiwan, on a Monday and check in at the elegant Grand Hotel. But when we ask for a double bed, the receptionist turns us down. As we are not yet married, they will only put us in a room with two single beds.

But we are married, we're married, I fib.

No, you are not. Your passports are different. You show us marriage certificate.

I look at Robert: Well? And he says, Do you want to get married here?

All right, I say.

We can get married in a Buddhist ceremony, Robert says, his eyes sparkling.

Robert is very romantic about it all. He takes charge, arranging for us to meet with the abbot of Taiwan. I don't know how we find him, but we do.

Abbot Tao An speaks a little English and seems fascinated by this young Australian couple who want to get married in Taiwan. We meet him on the Monday and he agrees to perform the wedding on the Wednesday. Which leaves Tuesday to prepare. Everyone from the temple is excited: Let's plan a wedding! And so they do.

On Wednesday morning, I choose an exquisite red hand-embroidered skirt and a cream blouse for my wedding outfit. I wear my hair flowing around my shoulders and slip a couple of gold bangles over my hand. As I'm getting ready, I think, This is the start of me having my own family and Robert will be a part of it.

It is 22 May 1974 and our ceremony is at 10 am at the Buddhist Soong Shan Temple's Precious Hall of the Dharma-raja. At the temple, Robert and I are given chocolate-brown robes to wear over our clothes. As we walk into the temple for the ceremony, there is a moment of madness as firecrackers explode all over the place. Newspapers back home report the curiosity of two Aussies marrying in such foreign circumstances.

The ceremony is all in Mandarin. Robert and I kneel before Abbot Tao, taking it all very seriously. We say our parts in English. I have a beautiful piece of old jade that I give Robert in place of a wedding ring, and he wears it around his neck.

Our wedding certificates are presented to us in a pretty red box – everything is in Chinese characters except for our names – and then it is time for the reception: a vegetarian feast attended by 200 of our nearest and dearest we have never met before.

For the next week we are the biggest celebrities in Taipei. Few Australians visit Taiwan, let alone marry in a Buddhist ceremony, so we are in the local papers and everywhere we go, we are given the royal treatment. Strangers come up to us with gifts. And, of course, when we return to the Grand Hotel after our reception the staff have already moved us into a new room. Ahhh, now you get double bed.

We are silly with love and our newfound fame when we fly out of Taipei for Japan. Our first stop in Tokyo is the Australian consulate. Now that we are married, I am not going to waste a moment changing my name. I want a new passport that says Donna Ehrenburg. Ehrenburg is better than Davis. I can erase Lois Davis once and for all.

I tell the consulate official all about our wedding in Taiwan and show her the marriage certificate, which looks a lot like a menu from a Chinese restaurant. She just looks at me and says, No, I am sorry, the marriage is not legal. The Australian Government will not recognise the marriage.

I can't believe it. All that for nothing?

So how do we make it legal? I ask.

You will have to go to the Japanese registry office and you will have to get married again.

Fine.

We find the registry office and we spend all day just queuing and hanging around – No, no, you just wait – and it is unbelievably frustrating, so Robert and I end up having a huge fight right there in the waiting room. Finally, a Japanese woman comes out and says, So you want to marry him?

Yes.

And you want to marry her?

Yes.

Okay, you are married now. One moment, please.

She returns with some forms, which we sign and take back to the Australian consulate.

Are we married now?

Yes, you are married.

CHAPTER 13

In Hong Kong, we rent an apartment near the Observatory on the Kowloon side. For reasons we can't figure out, it is very cheap. We take modelling jobs that pay cash and find a Seventh Day Adventist hospital where I will have the baby. We catch ferries everywhere, and in our free time we walk along the beach, go to see Chinese movies – indulging Robert's passion for martial arts – and dine out at all the Buddhist vegetarian restaurants. The food is sublime.

In our apartment, late at night we tune into the strange comings and goings in our building. We strain our eyes peering through the security hole in our door: heavily made-up girls in stilettos with men in business suits. Nobody ever stays long. And that's how we come to realise that we are living in the middle of a brothel; the other apartments are all filled with prostitutes. Oh well, I think, who cares? The apartment's in a great position and we are surrounded by gardens.

I love every minute of Hong Kong, but as our baby's birth approaches, I decide I want to go home.

We fly back to Melbourne. It is the height of spring, the flowers are in glorious bloom, and as the city gears up for the

Melbourne Cup I prepare to give birth. With nowhere else to go, we move in with Muffy and Ko in Warrandyte, a pretty suburb in the bushy outskirts of Melbourne. Fortunately, we don't have to break the news to them that we are married because they have already seen the newspaper story that came out after the wedding in Taiwan. Apparently, when Muffy read it she said to Robert's sister, Catherine, I will never shed another tear for that boy. She must have forgotten about that, though, because she accepts us into her home and she and I begin a bumpy ride to reconciliation.

My time in Asia has influenced the way I want to have the baby. I would like everything as loving and relaxed for the baby and me as possible. I could not bear another traumatic experience with my feet in stirrups and a nurse holding me down, chastising and shushing me. This time, the baby will be born my way.

I do some research and opt for a version of the Leboyer method, which is still quite revolutionary. The idea is that you minimise the stress of the birth and so create a more pleasant environment and a contented baby. The room you give birth in is quiet and dimly lit, and you can get into water to help with the pain. When the baby is born, it is gently massaged and then placed on your stomach to help you bond.

After seven hours of labour, my exquisite little boy is born at 4.15 pm on 11 November 1974, in the Seventh Day Adventist hospital in Warburton, with Robert by my side. I don't know whether it is the Leboyer method or just his nature, but he is the loveliest, calmest baby boy. We call him Dylan Jacobus, following the Dutch tradition of naming a child after their grandparent.

It is so different from when I had Wayne – I suppose because I have Robert and I have been out in the world. I have learnt how to love and Robert loves me. I bond with Dylan right from the start. Dylan is my precious little boy and I love him. I want to be the perfect mother. The nurses are so patient, teaching me how to breastfeed, showing me the way.

We bring Dylan home from the hospital and Ko just loves him too. In his very Dutch accent he takes to calling out, Where is my Dildo? We never have the heart to tell him what he is actually saying. He and Dylan become extremely close.

Now Muffy has something new to nag me about. You feed that baby at 10 pm, then you put him in his cot and you don't go back to him until the morning. Don't you spoil that baby.

So I put him in his bed, and I lie there listening to him crying and screaming and sobbing. It is awful. Every fibre of my being wants to pick him up and put him to my breast, but Muffy is spying on me. Don't you go near him. He's spoilt!

How can you spoil a newborn baby? I keep thinking.

When I am sure she is not looking, I sneak in to check on him. One time I get to his room to find he has been crying so much that he has his head wedged through the iron bars of his cradle. It is awful. My screams bring Robert running in, and he must have superhuman strength because he pulls the bars apart and frees Dylan. I shudder to think what would have happened had I not gone in.

I storm upstairs and Muffy knows it is bad. I stand over her and I say, Today is the last day you will tell me how to raise my child. From now on I am going to trust my instincts. And you will not interfere again.

She doesn't interfere after that.

Dylan is about six months old when I discover I am pregnant again. Robert wants me to have an abortion. He says it is too soon after Dylan, and I won't be able to manage. I do as he asks.

I never forgive him for that, actually. It is terrible. I can't bring myself to recall the details.

I decide the best way to get over the abortion is to start working. It will keep me occupied, not to mention help pay the bills. We have to start thinking about getting our own place. I have never liked relying on other people for a roof over my head. It reminds me too much of being a Welfare kid. The nuns at St Aidan's always used to say the only way to guarantee your future was to buy your own home. Otherwise, you could be thrown out on the street with not a moment's notice. And from my experience, they were right.

Robert has taken a job as a salesman with 3M and I have decided not to go back to modelling since having Dylan. A friend of mine sells flowers for a living, so I decide that could be a good job for me, too.

We are at the Footscray markets at 4 am Thursdays, Saturdays and Sundays, filling my baskets with flowers. Robert and Dylan come along as we drive around delivering the flowers to shops. Sometimes we set up a roadside stall. The business does well enough that soon we can afford to buy a delivery truck. We have our own little mobile florist.

We run the flower business at the weekends, and during the week I work nights as a waitress. I have to hire a nanny to help with Dylan. Buying a house is just so important to me.

Dylan is about one when we find a place we can afford in Canterbury Road, Toorak – a fabulous little weatherboard terrace with a huge living area and a backyard. Owning our own home is a great achievement. For the first time, I have a wonderful sense of security. Life is better than I could ever have hoped. Robert and I are in love and he brings a calmness that I need. He is also fun, having a great sense of humour. He will stick jelly beans up his nose just to make Dylan and me laugh.

Dylan is around three when Robert and I decide to try for another baby. I am thrilled when I fall pregnant almost straightaway.

I go back to the obstetrician who delivered Dylan, and we plan for another Leboyer birth. My belly pops out much earlier this time and by about four or five months I am huge. I just think, Well, it's my third baby, but when the doctor sees me, he says, I think we need to send you to the hospital for some bed rest. I think you might be working too hard.

I go to the Women's Hospital, where they examine me and discover that the umbilical cord is hanging out. It had been around the baby's neck and detached. The baby is no longer alive.

They tell me I will have to give birth to the baby now, and they induce me. Before long I am hit by full-blown labour – massive contractions and terrible diarrhoea – only with none of the motivation to make it through to the end.

I am in labour for hours and the baby won't come out. There is so much pain. They examine me again and when they realise I have suffered enough, they decide to give me pethidine. Why they didn't give it to me hours before, I don't know. Within minutes I am in la-la land. I even say to Robert, Go home. I'll be fine. Don't worry.

Are you sure?

Poor Robert has been holding my hand while I have been vomiting and crying and in agony for hours, trying to give birth, and now I am telling him, No no, this is fine, I'm happy now.

So, Robert leaves for a break but then the doctors come in and they say, Donna, what we have to do now is get the baby out.

I am so drugged up at this point that I am thinking, No problem, get it out.

A doctor explains, It's not very nice – what we have to do to you. We have to use our fists to push down on your stomach, and push the baby out.

Because I can't push anymore. I have nothing left.

So I am lying there and I take a deep breath and they push. And they push this poor little baby out of me.

It's a boy.

That is the hardest thing to do, give birth to a dead baby.

I don't get to hold him. They take him away immediately. I don't see him. No funeral, nothing. He is gone.

It only really hits me the next day. Oh my God, what have I been through? Suddenly I have a desperate urge to get out. I am back in the orphanage. Bed after bed after bed. I feel trapped, I have to plan my getaway. I am too scared to tell them I want to leave. I can hear babies crying, and I am thinking, I'm outta here.

So I quietly slip out of bed and head towards the lift, but the matron can see where I am going and she comes after me. Get back into bed! And I am so desperate, terrified that they will get hold of me again. The lift doors are closing and I am freaking out. It is like I am escaping from the orphanage. I tear into the lift as if I am on the run again. Get downstairs fast as I can, out on the street – oh, hell, I've got to get home. Into a taxi, still in my dressing gown. Don't stop, don't look around, just get me home. Back to Toorak, don't have any keys, jump the fence, break into the house.

Phew, I'm home.

But it is not enough. I want my baby. I can't stand everyone coming to visit and all the sympathy nonsense. It makes it worse. It is the start of three very black months of depression. I just sit in my chair for hours at a time, doing nothing, numb. I suppose I don't know how to deal with my grief. Robert is upset about the baby too, but I suspect he is more worried about my mental state.

Anything you want, he tells me, we will do it.

I want to run away again.

Within six weeks, we have rented out the house and are travelling around Asia.

*

In Japan, I try to model, but this time it all just seems too hard. So when one of us is needed back in Australia to deal with the house, which we've rented out, and its tenant, I volunteer to make the trip home while Robert and Dylan stay in Tokyo.

I am away for a few weeks sorting out our affairs, and when it is time to fly back to Japan, I think, I'll just surprise him. It is only when I arrive at the airport in Tokyo that I phone Robert and tell him I am here.

Where?

Narita.

Oh. Oh, oh, okay, I'll come and get you.

No, it'll cost you a fortune. It's okay, I'll just get a taxi and I will see you at home.

Oh, oh. Okay.

I can hear the panic in his voice.

My taxi pulls up outside the apartment block where we are staying, and Robert is standing out on the road with his arms folded. What on earth is going on with you? I ask.

Nothing.

Yes there is. You're having an affair, aren't you? You've been with someone else.

No, no, no.

Of course I know what's going on anyway, but I say, You tell me the truth now or I am going to start screaming. (It is pretty late at night.) I don't care. I will start screaming. Tell me the truth, I'll find out anyhow.

There is nothing going on.

Okay then, it's been nearly three weeks since we've had sex, so let's go to bed. I'll know if you're having an affair.

So he finally says, Yeah, I've been having an affair with a French girl.

My stomach lurches, but I am not going to show Robert how much he has hurt me.

119

All right, I say, you've got a week. You either come with me – and I am taking Dylan – or you run off with your little French floozy, and I go back to Australia and live in the house. So go on, go and do whatever you have to do and I will wait here.

So that's what he does. And he comes back.

I am still shattered, but there is a bizarre upside to his affair. It absolutely reinvigorates our sex life. There is nothing like knowing your partner has been with someone else to get your sex life going. Maybe it is the idea that someone else finds him attractive. It turns me on.

We come home and decide to try to conceive again. I really want another baby. A girl. I douche with diluted vinegar and eat all alkaline foods, which you're supposed to do to help conceive a girl – milk, meat, fish and no salt. I learn about family planning and follow the Billings method, knowing just the right time to make love. Robert is always on standby, ready to go for it and laughing at the same time. Come on, Robert, let's do it again to be sure, I say to him. Then I lie in bed with my hips in the air, not wanting to get up.

I fall pregnant and on 6 December 1979 my daughter is born at St Vincent's Private in Melbourne. I can't believe that I have done it. She is so beautiful, with thick black hair. Robert fills my room with yellow roses and we just stare at this little wonder.

She looks like a Jessica, and from the first moments of her life she and I are very close. The nurses want to take her to the nursery overnight but I won't let them. I can't take my eyes off her. She sleeps in her bassinette next to my bed so that when I fall asleep her fingers are wrapped around mine.

Jessie is the perfect baby. So cute, so contented. She just feeds and goes back to bed. Never cries. Robert and I have caring for her down to a fine art. Jessie wakes and he puts her on my breast.

She gulps the milk down; a little glutton. Robert knows when to switch her to the other side. I fall asleep again and he changes her and puts her back to bed.

I am so happy. Poor Dylan can't come to the hospital because he has chickenpox, but I have my beautiful son and now my girl. I can take care of her the way I always wanted someone to look after me.

I feel a little sad, too. When I look at Jessie I think about myself as a baby and I can't understand how my mother rejected me.

Robert and I are looking around for a new business venture when a friend suggests we open a vegetarian restaurant. We hire him to help set the place up and be our chef, and not long after Jessie is born, we open Mr Natural, a vegetarian pizza place in Chapel Street, South Yarra. A pie without a top, is our slogan. Wholemeal pizzas, everything natural, organic, all from scratch. It is right around the corner from the orange people, so is in a great position for a vegetarian restaurant.

We work long, frenetic hours; Robert makes pizzas while I take orders in between keeping an eye on Jessie, asleep in the flat upstairs. Then once the restaurant takes off, I am able to work less, so I am at home to tuck the children into bed.

Early one evening the next summer, around the time of Jessie's first birthday, I am at home with the kids while Robert is at work, when I notice Jessie is very quiet. She has had diarrhoea during the afternoon and now she is burning up. I ring the hospital and they tell me to try to bring her temperature down and to keep an eye on her. If she starts to have convulsions, bring her into the hospital, they say.

Soon Jessie starts to twitch and next thing I see her in bed jerking and shaking. I ring the ambulance, freaking out on the phone while they try to tell me what to do with her. Then Robert walks in the door, and I just throw Jessie at him. She's swallowed her tongue! He is running up and down the hallway, repeating, She's dead, she's dead, the baby's dead, while I yell at him to put her down and take the phone so that the emergency operator can explain what to do.

The ambulance arrives and Jessie is rushed to hospital. When we arrive close behind the ambulance the nurse keeps asking, Has she been eating jelly? Has she been eating jelly? And I am saying, No, it's blood. It's blood!

Jessie is bleeding from the bowel.

It turns out Jessie has salmonella, a type of food poisoning, in her bowel. The majority of people get salmonella in the stomach, but if you get it in the bowel it is quite serious. Jessie is still being breastfed, so I cannot figure out how it happened, except that yesterday she was crawling around with another baby and, being summer, they were both naked. All I can think is that some faeces from the other baby must have gotten in her mouth.

My little girl goes into shock and is very sick for about three weeks. She doesn't recognise Robert or me. She is just lying in that hospital bed and we are numb with the fear of losing her. We stay every minute at the hospital, touching her and giving her the will to live. I wonder about the times when I was a little girl in the Children's Hospital with my tummy problems and bowel surgery. Apparently, I took a long time to heal and I am sure it was because there was no one there to love me. This thought helps me love Jessie even more.

She slowly pulls through and when at last she recognises me, I know she is on the mend. But the doctors are concerned that because she had a seizure she is now at risk of developing epilepsy, particularly if there is any epilepsy in the family. I am terrified, thinking back to stories of my mother's fits and my sister Mary who was sent to a mental hospital. But I don't say anything about it. I have never told anyone about the epilepsy in my family, not even Robert. I can't. For some reason it humiliates me too much.

At last we take Jessie back home and she is getting better, but then one day we are at the park when she has another seizure. I take her to our family doctor, John Officer, a distinguished older gentleman. He explains that yes, something like what Jessie has been through can trigger epilepsy. I am sitting there thinking, Well, it's definitely in the genes. I know I have to tell him but, bloody hell, it is hard. Eventually I say, I'm really embarrassed by this, but there is epilepsy in my family.

And he just says, Donna, my daughter's an epileptic. There is nothing to be ashamed of. It's okay.

It is silly, but I feel that if he is this well-known doctor in Toorak and his daughter has epilepsy and it is okay, then maybe my family is not so bad.

Dr John puts Jessie on an anti-convulsant drug for six months and, thank God, everything is fine. She doesn't develop epilepsy. But her recovery is slow and she is weak for a long time. She becomes so clumsy she will trip over a tissue. We have come too close to losing her already and I am not going to lose another child. My babies' health comes first, so I decide we have to get them out of the city. Take their shoes off and let them run around in the bush.

We sell the restaurant and the house, only holding on to an investment property we've acquired which is bringing in rent money. And while Robert finalises our affairs in Melbourne, Muffy, the kids and I fly north to Noosa, on Queensland's Sunshine Coast, looking for somewhere to live.

Scarlet is in Byron Bay, four hours' drive south of Noosa in far north New South Wales – she owns a milk bar there – and I am desperate to spend time with her, so we hire a car and head down to stay with her for a while. I have been up this way once before, when I went to the Aquarius Festival in Nimbin in the early seventies. I stayed for a few nights in a caravan park in Byron and was instantly attracted to the town. Even then I decided I would like to live here one day.

Byron Bay is little more than a seaside village of surfers, hippies and escapees from the city. A small group of locals and only a few tourists living amongst the weatherboard houses, frangipanis and bougainvillea. It is idyllic. I find a wonderful old house – weatherboard, of course, with wide verandahs – on Old Bangalow Road, with breathtaking views over Broken Head. It is close to the town and minutes to the beach. The day I inspect it, I buy it.

That night I ring Robert back in Melbourne. I thought I'd better congratulate you, I say. You bought a house today. You'd better come up.

CHAPTER 14

Getting Jessie in touch with the earth does wonders for her and within a year she is a normal, healthy little girl. Robert and I don't have jobs, but we have the rent from our remaining Melbourne property plus our savings. We are happily married, Dylan has started school and the kids are thriving. It is 1982. Within the year I am pregnant again and preparing for another baby.

I am about four months along when the complications begin. There is some bleeding and some contractions and I end up in hospital in Lismore, where they tell me that I have an incompetent cervix; they need to stitch, otherwise the baby could fall out. Before they do that, though, they need to check that the baby is all right, so they are sending me to Brisbane for an amniocentesis. They start making arrangements for a helicopter to fly me there, but when they realise I don't have private health insurance they tell me I will have to make my own way. I go home and prepare to make the three-hour drive the next day.

At home that night, though, I go to the toilet and when I pull down my pants, there is the baby. In my underpants. It has just fallen out. I sit there and call out to Robert. He wraps the baby in a towel and takes us to the hospital.

I am given a bed and my wonderful doctor comes to see me. He holds my hand and says, I am really sorry, Donna. You've just had a little boy, and he is beautiful.

He is so patient with me, so kind. He just says, There was nothing wrong with him. You'll be able to have another baby.

I go home but two days later I am back on the toilet, bleeding heavily. Robert and the kids are out, so I get myself to the telephone to ring the hospital. The bleeding won't stop – not pouring out but pulsating. Cuploads. I get through to the hospital: Oh my God, I am in a bad way. I'm bleeding pretty bad.

How heavy is the bleeding?

A towel doesn't seem to help anymore. It's all over the floor.

You'd better lie down and we'll get an ambulance up there.

It's a funny thing with haemorrhaging that you can feel fine. I actually have a shower because I am so embarrassed. The ambulance is coming and I want to make sure I am clean.

Robert arrives home, distressed to find me bleeding so heavily: What can I do? What can I do? Then the ambulance arrives.

At the hospital, the doctor wants to do a hysterectomy. He says my uterus has given up. But Robert says, I don't want her to have a scar.

So the doctor agrees first to try an old-fashioned treatment where they pack your uterus with weights. They string my legs up and pack my uterus and I am given twenty-four hours for the bleeding to stop. If it continues, the doctor will go ahead with the hysterectomy.

Fortunately, the bleeding stops. I am given a blood transfusion and spend a week in hospital before being sent home to recuperate. As we are leaving the hospital, the doctor says to Robert, Donna can never have another baby. She would never survive childbirth. She has already been through so much, I really think you should consider having a vasectomy.

I get very depressed after that. Because that is it. No more kids.

*

In the winter of 1983 we sell our house to Muffy and Ko, who move up to Byron Bay to be closer to us, and we buy a bigger house across the road. I think Muffy has come to like me – partly because there is no other grandmother for her to contend with. Robert thinks it's great, too, that he doesn't have to deal with a mother-in-law.

With our new house we have stepped up a notch. Now we live in a place where people think that we must be a bit rich. And Robert goes along with it. He is a great storyteller, Robert. When I first met him he had a picture of a Chinese girl torn from a magazine that he kept in his Mini Moke and said was his girl-friend. When we were travelling through Asia, I discovered she was a famous Chinese actress.

Robert might like people thinking that he is someone special, but the reality is that we are unemployed and on the dole. Welcome to Byron Bay.

I thoroughly resent this. To my mind it is like, Well, if I am on the dole I might as well be single. Because I really feel it is Robert's turn to support me and the kids. I have worked since I was a teenager. I have never had a man take care of me, never relied on the government since I ran away from my last institution. Even when I have been pregnant, no matter how many months pregnant, I have worked. I am not going to end up in an orphanage again and nor will my children. People say I am money driven, and maybe I am but you have to survive. I always have a fridge full of food so that the Welfare people cannot walk in and take my kids away.

What would give me the most pleasure in life is to die leaving my children money. To know that they each have a house; that would give me a lot of pleasure on my deathbed. But Robert won't work. Instead, he sits around reading while I worry about where the next dollar is coming from. And so the arguing starts. I am so tired, so depressed. I have just lost a baby, for God's sake. I am exhausted.

Deep down I think I blame Robert for a lot of things – because of the abortion years ago and because I have had to work so hard. It's not that Robert doesn't do anything; he helps with the kids and dusts the whole house every day. He makes sure any ornaments are centred and that books are lined up on the shelves with the other books of the same height. But with Robert everything is about show. How something looks is more important to him than what goes on behind the veneer. This stems from the same insecurity that drives his fear of someone discovering the truth about my childhood. I try to tell him: People don't care that I was an orphan. But it embarrasses him. He wants me to be something I'm not. Every day he still decides which clothes he wants me to wear and lays them out on the bed. It didn't bother me twelve years ago, but now I am sick of it. I want to discover myself, express myself. I no longer want to hide who I really am behind pretty baubles and a spotless house.

This all festers inside me and, despite my pleading, Robert still doesn't find work. Every day the tension grows until finally I tell him I am leaving. He has had a year to support me and has done nothing. I have lost respect for him. Of course, me being me, I want to do it all without emotions being involved. So I say, Right, I'll leave at the end of the week, but let's stay really calm about it and not worry the kids.

So, we agree to that. We won't upset the kids, we won't even tell them yet. But the day I am leaving, when I pull out the suitcase to start packing, Robert goes into meltdown. I think the reality hits him. He starts vomiting.

I cannot deal with confronting someone close to me so I immediately buckle: Don't worry, I won't leave. You can have one more year to start paying the bills.

*

I read an article in Robert's *Playboy* magazine that says if you do not have sex three times a week then your marriage is doomed. Our marriage is in serious trouble anyway, but it is certainly doomed according to that equation. We just don't have any passion. In the beginning we did, of course. But after twelve years it is like we are brother and sister, except that we are raising a couple of kids and paying off a mortgage. People even tell us we look like siblings. I lie in bed at night wishing that Robert would kiss me passionately.

I tell him of my need for passion. I am becoming very dissatisfied and it is a feeling I long to escape – I need someone who is strong and down to earth. In desperation, Robert suggests I have an affair. He doesn't want me to but he says, Go and do it if you have to. Get it out of your system. Just don't leave me. I don't want to lose you.

It is not that I want to hurt Robert. He has always been good to me; he's not a drinker, he's not violent, which has been great for twelve years. But now I am finding out who I am and discovering new needs and desires. At this point – even though I know rationally what a destructive, last-ditch effort this would really be – an affair seems the only alternative to divorce.

I am so lonely and I feel like love is the only cure for my loneliness. I am so sad, I feel that only my soul can do the crying for me. I suddenly know how much crying I have in me. As much as I want to forget about my past, I can't. I still have nightmares, waking with the fear of being caught, and leaping out of bed in the middle of the night. Robert never knows what is going on because we never talk about my childhood.

There is a friend of ours, Bruce, who I have always really liked, and I can tell he is quite keen on me. So when Bruce next comes up to Byron Bay to stay with us, I think, This could be the man I have the affair with. Even Robert says to me, Bruce likes you. Robert says he would actually prefer me to have the affair with one of our friends.

Part of me feels like a tramp but also excited. I have a sense of independence, freedom. Late one evening, when Bruce and I are still up, I tell him I want to make love. He responds warmly and things start to happen between us. That night I have sex with him downstairs while my husband is asleep upstairs. I feel sick about it, but strangely, it feels good, too. Somebody else wants me after twelve years. It isn't love, though, it is just sex and I wonder how can I have betrayed Robert? I keep thinking back to when we were in Japan and the girl he betrayed me with. Is this payback?

Bruce and I are only together the once. The guilt is too much to bear.

While all this has been going on, the Victorian Government has passed a *Freedom of Information Act* in 1982, which entitles citizens to access their records from the government. It occurs to me that I could probably apply for my file from the Welfare Department.

I deliberate over the decision for almost a year. Part of me feels I need something from my childhood, some sort of proof that it happened so that perhaps I can finally let it go. But the bigger, more dominant part of me is saying, No way. Absolutely not. Why would I want to bust open those old wounds? Why would I want to bring up everything I have spent half my life trying to hide? Robert does not know what my mother is like. He doesn't know what went on at the orphanage, that I have a sister who, even now, is in a mental institution, or that there is a family history of epilepsy. How could I possibly tell him all this after the way he and his family reacted when they discovered I was an orphan?

Towards the end of 1983, I am in Melbourne without Robert and the kids when a friend encourages me just to go ahead and make an application for the file. So, on a whim, I do.

The file reaches Byron Bay on a day I am out. It is addressed to me but Robert decides to go ahead and open it himself. I arrive home to discover him and his mother reading the fat stack of photocopies. Robert just looks up at me and says, This came for you today.

I am devastated when I see them. I feel exposed and humiliated, the way I felt the whole time I was growing up.

Robert and Muffy are not at all sympathetic, particularly about my mother's history. The stuff about my mother is pretty bad: prostitution, men, mental illness. Robert is giving me a look of horror. He is ashamed of me. He does not want anyone to see who he has married. Even though I know he loves me, his attitude is, Never tell anyone. Don't talk about the orphanage stuff.

My life is not my own. I feel this irresistible need to run away and hide the way I did as a child. Only this time, I can stay away.

Robert's and my marriage had obviously been rocky before he and his mother read my file, but after that I know there is no possibility of reconciliation. I leave him in January 1984. I don't even tell him at first. I can't stand the thought of confrontation. I just go on a holiday and stay out of contact until he realises I am not coming back.

The kids remain with me and I take a second mortgage on the house in Byron Bay to pay Robert out. It is all reasonably amicable, as much as divorce can be, I suppose. Robert is a gentle person and I will always cherish what we had together.

Marriage to him and having our two children are the best things that have ever happened to me. Looking back, I am surprised the marriage lasted so long, given how damaged I am. It lasted as long as I felt safe that no one really knew about me, about how bad I was.

My marriage had given me security, and with that gone I feel very lost. I haven't experienced much outside Robert and his family and our children. Not in terms of men and relationships. In some ways, I am quite naïve.

I try to read the Welfare file myself but it is too much for me. I have spent years trying to erase all of that: the memories of Mary Fishpot; the truth about my mother. I cannot have come from a woman like Dorothy Davis. I have fantasy parents; they live in the country. I still tell everyone that.

So, the file is closed and put away in a bottom drawer. Even when I move house it always remains in a bottom drawer, locked away.

Little do I know that there is worse to come, many more bottom drawers to be filled. Before too long, buried deepest of all, will be a small, neat journal covered in woolly red fabric, containing secrets I won't share for many years.

I would never have broken up my marriage had I known what lay ahead.

CHAPTER 15

Dylan is nine and Jessie is four when we move back to Melbourne for a while. I have to distance myself from Robert while he is still angry at me for leaving him, and I want to move away from Muffy and Ko – it is hard enough living right near your in-laws when you are actually married.

Eventually, I sell the place in Byron Bay and buy a grand old Victorian house in South Yarra. A lovely home with two date palms out the front and a wide backyard. I work for a time as a nanny for a girlfriend's child before finding a job in publishing, at an in-house magazine. Robert comes and stays with us whenever he wants to see the children. There is no set plan, but it works for us. Once he gets over my leaving him, everything is reasonably relaxed. We even manage to hold on to a sense of family, which is important to me.

The end of my marriage, and being back in Melbourne, start me thinking about my mother. The kids have a right to meet their grandmother and once again I feel drawn to her. I discover that my cousin, Rhonda, who is a community nurse, had received a call to see an elderly lady who had fallen and needed help. Rhonda found the house in total disarray and as she was taking the woman's details, realised the woman was her mother's sister, Dorothy Davis. No one had heard from her in years. Rhonda arranged for her to be taken to a house in Armadale, with about ten other elderly women, which is where I find her. I take Dylan and Jessie. The three of us just stand at the end of her bed and look intently; I am always nervous when I see her and I don't know what to think or do. She never gets out of bed, never lifts her head to acknowledge her grandchildren. There is nothing physically wrong with her. I think she just feels sad and embarrassed. She has given up on life well before her time. We go back to see her every now and then. Sometimes I go alone. But she and I never really talk, never touch. I try to ask her about her life, her thoughts, but all she keeps saying is, Where is Scarlet?

In the end, she dies lonely and alone, barely raising her head to speak to anyone. The guilt or the pain catches up with her, I suppose. Poor thing.

Only after she is gone am I able to feel tenderness towards her. I wish I could have loved her. I never held her and she never held me. I was always too scared to get too near her. I wish someone could have helped her to help us kids.

We have been in Melbourne going on four years when – towards the end of 1987 – Dylan and Jessie start nagging me to move back to Byron Bay. They are pining for their friends and the freedom; the beaches and the running around. The two of them have been fighting constantly since I left Robert, and I think maybe a return north will improve the situation. Besides, I miss Byron myself.

We sell the house at the height of a boom and I nearly double our money in less than two years. It means I can afford to buy us a house in Byron Bay, put a deposit on an investment property, and even splurge on a red convertible BMW. In a lovely twist of serendipity, the first house we ever owned in Byron Bay is on the market and so we buy it back – from my ex-mother-in-law Muffy.

The kids are thrilled to be back home but they continue to drive each other mad. They have always fought but it is getting out of control. I simply cannot cope on my own anymore, so for the first time I begin to entertain the idea of separating them. I think it would be best for all of us if I sent one of them to live with their father, who is now living in Sydney.

Dylan is thirteen, and Jessie eight, going on eighteen. As he is older and less demanding, it makes more sense to send Dylan. He is entering adolescence and the whole Byron hippie scene and surf culture is beckoning. Plus, I simply cannot help him with his homework anymore. I never went to high school so I have no idea about the things he is learning. His father is a big reader and I know he will take the time to help Dylan.

I can justify my decision to send Dylan to live with his dad because at the time I really do not feel I have an option. It is about self-preservation and doing the best for my kids and me. But in my heart I will always regret doing it. It is gut-wrenching. He does not want to go. Even though I tell Dylan how much I miss him and love him, it brings back all those feelings of giving up Wayne. It breaks my heart to think that Dylan might for an instant believe I abandoned him.

Fortunately, Robert is thrilled to have Dylan, which makes it easier, and I think Dylan realises over time that I have our best interests at heart. Dylan is a wonderfully kind person and we are blessed to have a very close bond.

With Dylan in Sydney, for a while it is just Jessie and me. I begin dating again, falling into a whirlwind affair with a gregarious, handsome Legal Aid lawyer. But it is over almost before it begins when his infatuation with me turns violent; during a fiery argument he dangles me over a balcony and I know we can never stay together.

I am surprised, though, at the grief I feel over the end of the relationship. My attachment to this man is even stronger than I realised, and I struggle to find some peace in the aftermath. I keep myself busy taking care of Jessie and doing up an investment property I have bought in town. It is another old weatherboard on a corner block minutes from the beach – it is in a fabulous location but needs lots of work. The lino is horrible and the carpet filthy, the garden overgrown. I set about fixing it up.

I also become passionately involved in a campaign to save the sandhills and Byron Bay primary school. I join the Byron Bay Action Group, which is fighting to stop the council giving away the town's Memorial Recreation Grounds to use as a new primary school site. The Department of Education wants to build an ugly brick-veneer school on the beautiful grassy sandhills above the beach even though they already have a perfectly lovely school amongst the trees a couple of streets back. Everybody thinks, fabulous, a new school, but the sneaky thing is that once they rezone the rec grounds to build the school, it opens the door for more development to take place, paving the way for the whole shoreline to become cheek-by-jowl hotels.

Our efforts pay off. In the end, they decide to renovate the old school instead, which turns out to be the best thing for Byron Bay because we get a new school and still get to keep our sandhills and the park.

Through it all I discover how brutal politics can be. But I also discover that I have a power in me that I should use more. Being part of the Action Group gives me far more satisfaction than making money, as I enjoy being involved in something I feel so passionate about.

I continue working on the new house, which is starting to look quite lovely, and I pick up some part-time work as a journalist with the *Byron News*. Then, following on from our victory with the rec grounds, the chamber magistrate enlists my help to campaign for a new courthouse, which ends up being another success. I am thoroughly enjoying myself, plus it all helps to keep my mind off the lawyer I was involved with. I miss him terribly, even though I know he is no good for me.

More importantly, I feel as though there is some purpose emerging in my life. I am doing something with myself, which gives me a bit of credibility in the town. I no longer see myself as just an unloved orphan.

It is the winter of 1989 and I am tossing up whether I should get involved in local politics, or maybe pursue journalism. But no, what do I do? I meet Eddie.

CHAPTER 16

He is ten years younger than me; a tall, dark-haired, handsome and mysterious man, with an air of danger about him, who walks into my life and turns it upside down. We surprise each other.

Eddie Myatt has a sexy grin and the quiet, dark intensity that appeals enormously to the romantic side of my being. He is charming and free-spirited. Nothing like my lawyer boyfriend or Robert, who were always attempting to keep me in line. Eddie is a liberating force; he gives me back those years when it was okay to be reckless and spontaneous, although I suppose I never really learnt to play. But Eddie and I hang out and go to the beach. He is like a frisky puppy bouncing around me. Eddie sees the light side of life, and makes me laugh. His fun and spontaneity completely bowl me over.

He is a sannyasin, or one of the 'orange people', the term given to the orange-robed disciples of the famous Indian guru Bhagwan Rajneesh, nicknamed by the media 'the guru of the vagina'. Eddie has spent a lot of time in the Rajneeshi ashram in India, meditating and learning about the path to enlightenment. He teaches me to concern myself only with the things that I *can* do something about, and to laugh off the things I have no hope of changing.

St Aidan's, 1950.

ABOVE: *Me at nineteen years of age.*
RIGHT: *Starting my modelling career, 1970.*

Robert and I were twenty-one and twenty when this photo was taken — we had just met.

Jessie (aged two) always wanted to fly and Dylan was her protector.

Robert would do anything to make the kids laugh.

ABOVE: *Dylan (aged nine) in Bali.*
RIGHT: *Me, 1986.*

Eddie on the beach in Goa, India.

Harper, one month old.

Jessie (twelve) and Harper (six months) in Bali.

My 40th birthday celebrations, shortly after Harper was born.

Harper and me in Byron Bay, 1992.

Harper (aged ten)
after hang-gliding in
Byron Bay.

Dylan, sixteen
years old.

ABOVE: *Dylan*
(aged twenty-five)
and Robert.

RIGHT: *Jessie,*
sweet sixteen.

Harper and me.

My garden in Byron Bay.

Eddie is a hairdresser by trade, although he is not working much at the moment, so he is happy to pick up a hammer to help with the renovations at the corner house in town. He is very generous with his time. He paves the courtyard out the back, does the cooking, takes Jessie to school. He always arrives at my house with champagne and hash. I have never been much of a pot smoker – not since I was in St Kilda with Carmel when I was modelling – but the bubbles go to my head and being with Eddie makes everything more intoxicating. Soon he is spending so much time at my house he is virtually living with us. Jessie adores him, because he is young and cool. He drives her around in his green 1964 Holden.

I continue to agonise over my failed relationship with the lawyer. I can't seem to let him go; Eddie is the perfect distraction, I suppose. He seems besotted with me so it is easy to convince myself that I am falling in love with him too. Plus, he is sweeping me off my feet with his champagne and compliments. But the more we drink, the more I start to unravel; the more confused and emotional I feel. I have never had much of a tolerance for alcohol; then one night when Eddie and I have drunk too much champagne, he pulls out a small pill and asks if I would like to try it. He says it is ecstasy – which I have never had – and that I will really enjoy it. I am thirty-nine, for goodness sake. I have never tried any drugs other than alcohol and pot, but I am feeling reckless. Okay, I say.

Soon I start to feel very strange. Suddenly I want to talk about everything: my whole life, the orphanage. The next morning I wake up depressed. I don't know what I am doing with Eddie. Part of me is using him, part of me is infatuated with him. I have no doubt he is using me too. Someone tells me they bumped into him in the street and said to him, I hear you're going out with Donna. No, he replied, I'm having an affair with her BMW.

I try to break away from him a few times but he always

improves his behaviour, tells me he needs me, and I forgive him. I am vulnerable and he is available. My emotional attachment to him is very strong. It clouds my viewpoint.

In October 1989 I decide to go to Bali with a girlfriend. Get some distance between Eddie and me, work out what I really want. I have only been with him a few months but, as usual with me, things are very intense.

I book my ticket to Indonesia, but then Eddie asks me to travel with him instead. You've been to Bali before, he says. Let me take you to Goa in India. It is the most beautiful place, with wonderful stone houses near the beach. I love you, Donna. I will take care of you. Please come with me.

It does sound wonderful. Eddie says this trip is just what we need. We will go for a few months, travel on to London and Amsterdam and all these exotic places I have only dreamt about. Things between us will improve once we leave Byron Bay and all the drama behind us. So I cancel my ticket to Bali, arrange for Jessie to go and stay with Robert for a while, and we book two world tickets. First stop: Bombay.

Only after I have agreed to go, does Eddie tell me he is going to have to sell his old Holden to cover the cost of his ticket. He feels really bad about it because that car has been in his family for twenty years. His father gave it to him three years ago and Eddie has put all his spare cash and time into restoring it.

Poor Eddie loves that car so much and he seems really upset at the prospect of parting with it. So I offer to 'buy' the car from him in return for the fare to India on the understanding that as soon as he can repay me, he can buy the car back. I put both tickets on my credit card.

Our flights are booked out of Melbourne, so in mid-October we head south and finalise our travel arrangements from there.

Eddie says we are better off taking gold, rather than Australian dollars, to India. He says you can't get a good exchange rate for the Aussie dollar over there, but we can double our money on the gold. With all those bangles and ornaments the women wear, gold is better than money. And once we have sold it, we can buy US dollars. Eddie says this is what he does whenever he goes to India. It is very common, apparently. And this way he will be able to pay me back for the car as soon as we are in India. We purchase the gold from a bullion dealer in Elizabeth Street.

There is one last thing I want to do before we leave. I need to see my father, to forgive him. I thought I would never forgive him, but he is getting old and I can't live with the anger anymore.

I am still in touch with my half-brothers and sisters – I am actually closer to them than to my full sisters – and they lead me to my father in Coburg. He is sick with emphysema, hooked up to oxygen tanks. I feel sorry for him. At last I put my arms around him and we talk.

Once he starts talking he can't stop. I can see his desperation. This need to communicate with me. I have tormented him all these years with my silence and now he can see he finally has a chance. He must be thinking, She is actually listening. He tells me about the family, the old days in the bush. I can see he hasn't got long to live and there is so much I want to know. I want to know stories about him and my mother. How they met, how they could have left us kids. I suppose that is what riles me to this day, that they robbed me of growing up with a family.

The only thing I don't discuss with him is what happened in the car when I first met him. I have never told anyone. I should talk to him about it. I would like to, but . . .

Six weeks later my father passes away. I feel sad. I think I made peace with him, I am just sorry we were never close. I could not look him in the face. He was a strange man, a father to eleven children.

You should never have left me in an orphanage, Dad.

I have told Jessie I will keep a journal for her while I am away, so that later on she and Dylan can read all about my travels. I buy a pretty little notebook, covered in woolly red fabric.

On 31 October 1989, we fly out of Melbourne for Bombay.

CHAPTER 17

```
For Jessica
For you to read at your leisure.
Love your Mother, India
My trip, 1989
```

The first few weeks in Goa are magical: long, sun-drenched days on the beach, good food and the best massages in the world to ease you into cloudless nights of music and laughter . . . wonderful.

Eddie sells our gold for US currency, which earns us a tidy little profit, and we rent a couple of rooms in a guest house in Calangute, hippie central on the shores of the Arabian Sea. There are no large buildings, just the odd stone house here and there. The Portuguese influence is everywhere, from the houses to the rich, spicy food. We eat every meal out, I don't have to clean or cook; there is nothing to do but lie on the beach and wander the streets of beautiful Goa.

25.11.89

. . . lying once again on the beach, eating so well, trying to be at peace within myself, is it possible? Who knows. I watch Ed meditating wondering what it's doing for him. I think I realised in Bombay he is just not in love with me. In words, yes, but actions, no.

Every day goes by & I think, Jessie's birthday soon. I hope you got the telegram.

4 Dec

Sometimes I wonder if I should give you this book. I write silly things at times. Soon we will be going to Amsterdam . . .

Travelling this time for me brings back lots of memories [of] when I travelled with Robert. Eddie is a lot like your dad, very gentle and easygoing. I have to stop myself from calling him Robert from time to time. Jessie, I want you to know I loved your dad very much, he was very good to me. The times we spent together were and are some of my most treasured moments. I will always hold a small place in my heart for him. You could never have had a better dad . . .

6th Dec. 89

Happy Birthday Darling Jessica . . .

Today I feel very sick. My body needs to rest . . .

Despite the change of scenery, things with Eddie continue to go up and down. He has friends here, other sannyasins, and he spends most of his time hanging out with them, getting stoned.

He is pretty self-absorbed. He carries around an envelope full of photographs of himself.

I sense there is something not quite right going on with him. There is a cat-and-mouse game playing out between us; when I am clingy and loving he doesn't want me but when I detach myself and act unavailable he suddenly decides he wants me again.

It all makes me feel more vulnerable than ever; I don't have my kids with me, I don't have my own house. I feel as though I have lost my power.

8.12.89
How long can one lie on the beach read eat & sleep. It's now five weeks & I've had enough. I want to get out. I'm bored. I need people & life around me. I'm sick of looking at the same faces. Goa is beautiful, so is Byron. Byron Bay - how lucky we are to have such a nice space to live.

I can't shake off this sickness. I am dizzy and nauseated and it is getting worse. All of a sudden everything is unbearable. Eddie is spending too much money on dope, the food tastes different. I can't stand Eddie touching me; my breasts are tender and I feel depressed.

Eddie is always out, and when he comes back to the house he is stoned and secretive. He is pulling away from me and I can feel myself becoming more emotionally erratic as I try to cling to him. I miss Jessie and Dylan. Why am I even here?

I tell Eddie I want to go to Amsterdam but he says he is not interested in leaving India. He wants to go to the Rajneeshi ashram in Poona, the home of the sannyasins. (It is only a month before Bhagwan Rajneesh dies in Poona.)

Okay, I say, even though that is not what I want to do. We are given an AIDS test before they will let us into the ashram.

After a few days in Poona, I have had enough. All I want to do is go home and be with my children for Christmas. The sannyasins depress me with their naïve, forced joyousness. I am physically drained and Eddie is still remote. The ashram has a strange effect on him; even apart from the amount of ecstasy and hash he has been taking, he seems to be undergoing enormous changes. He tells me that he has met a man he is physically attracted to. He isn't sure if it is the dope playing tricks on him or whether his feelings are genuine. Everything is coming apart.

I tell him that whether or not he comes with me, I am returning to Australia. It is only once I have given him the ultimatum I realise I really do want him to come with me. I love him. I need him to love me.

We have some terrible arguments in the last days in Poona. I am getting worse physically and Eddie is taking more and more drugs. I plead with him to come home to Australia where we can sort things out. I tell him I want a chance to make things more stable for us.

He finally agrees to fly home with me.

We return to Bombay and I head straight to the airport to change our tickets. We will fly out in the morning. My ticket is booked to return to Sydney, so I can go straight to see the kids, and Eddie is booked to go on to his family in Melbourne.

Despite what I have said to him, I realise this is probably the end for Eddie and me. Once I get off that plane in Sydney without him, I think it will be final.

We have stopped for a coffee at the airport when, out of the blue, Eddie says, Since we're going back to Australia, I want to take some hash with me.

Don't worry, he adds, I've done it heaps of times.

Even taking into account the amount of dope he has been smoking, I can't believe what he is saying. Are you serious? I ask.

Yeah, it's fine.

He is acting so cool about it, completely dispassionate.

No, Eddie, I say, I don't want to know about this.

I'm the one doing it, he says, not you.

I don't put up an argument. I don't have the energy. I just want to get home and see my kids.

We check in at a hotel near the airport for the night and Eddie disappears. He returns at around 11 pm with some slabs of black hash, I don't know how many, but they are about the length of a shoebox. I have never seen so much hash before.

He starts pulling all this gear out of a black suitcase and laying it on the table. Scissors, beeswax, pins, tape. He is totally calm. He says he does this all the time. It is perfectly safe, he reckons.

Stop worrying, Donna, he keeps telling me. It has nothing to do with you.

I just want to go back to sleep but instead I keep my eyes on Eddie to see what he is planning.

He starts chopping the hash into small pieces. They look like chocolate bullets. Then, one at a time, he sticks a pin in each bullet of hash, dips it in the melted beeswax, waits a few minutes for it to set and then dips it again. It is a ritual. I am absolutely amazed at how experienced he seems to be at this. And then when he has all these hard little bullets lined up, he starts swallowing them. God only knows how he does such a thing, but I watch him do it. He washes them down with water as though they are nothing more than painkillers. I can't help thinking about what it must do to his stomach, all that beeswax and hash. He must swallow around a kilo of the stuff, which seems to me to be like trying to park a semi-trailer in a one-car garage.

Even after Eddie has swallowed that much hash there is still loads of it left. He cuts that into smaller blocks, wraps it in the brown tape and packs it away in his suitcase.

The next morning, we pack up and Eddie gets the luggage into a taxi while I go downstairs and pay the bill. Even on the way to the airport he washes down more of his little bullets.

We are seated right up the back of the plane, jammed in to the centre block. I don't know what is wrong with me but I still feel sick. Tired and teary. We have something to eat and then Eddie hands me some Valium pills. Here, these will make you feel better.

I have never taken Valium before. Eddie says these are much stronger than what you get in Australia. Ten milligrams each. I take two pills and all the tension washes away. I am so relaxed, and then I am asleep.

I am woken by Eddie talking to me and the attendants bringing around tea. I feel dreadful; nauseated and disoriented. How long have I been asleep?

Eddie tells me we are only a couple of hours away from Sydney. I have slept right through the stopover in Singapore. I want to go back to sleep but Eddie wants to talk. It seems urgent. He is acting strange, whispering. I have to concentrate through the Valium haze to understand what he is saying.

Have you ever been searched going through Customs? he wants to know.

No.

Women very rarely get body-searched, he says. Have you ever been body-searched?

No, never.

He takes my hand.

Donna, you know I really love you, don't you, he says. Do you love me?

Well, I left my children at home to be with you.

He is all soft now, stroking me, loving me. It feels good. He hasn't been like this since we arrived in India.

You know, Donna, if you really loved me you would do this one thing for me.

What thing?

I've got all this hash in my bag but I don't look straight enough to get it through. Look at me. They'll stop me for sure.

Suddenly he seems vulnerable, nervous. His drug-taking has taken its toll. He tells me how safe it is. Everything will be okay. They never search girls. Just do this one thing for me.

No way, I say. I told you I didn't want to know anything about this. Don't ask me to do this. Don't do this to me.

Please do this for me, Donna, I've got to get on my feet. (He is pleading now.) I'm sick of people calling me your toy boy. For Christ's sake, give me a break. Let me set myself up without relying on you. Don't you see I'd be able to love myself more if I was financially independent? I need this.

I want nothing to do with the drugs, but then Eddie says, what it comes down to is this: if you love me, you will do it.

How would we do it? I eventually ask.

We'll go into the toilet and I can give it to you. It won't be a problem.

I don't know how to respond.

You've got nothing to worry about, Donna. I promise I will take care of you.

I don't know . . .

Come on, Donna. This will be so good for me. I'll have my own money and I won't have to rely on you. We can get a house together and start over. I'll be better, I promise.

I feel my resistance ebbing away. I am too sick and tired to argue. I want him to know that I love him. I don't want him to leave me.

So Eddie goes to the toilet and a couple of minutes later I follow him in.

Eddie locks the door behind me and pulls out a package wrapped in brightly coloured Indian paper. He unwraps the parcel and removes several tightly packed packages wrapped in masking tape.

As he hands over the slabs of hash, I quietly start to cry. I do not want to be doing this, but at the same time I want to prove my love to him. He says I am doing the right thing and that we are going to be so happy together.

He is more confident now, instructing me on the plan. Since I am bringing the hash in and I am getting off in Sydney, he will now have to leave the flight in Sydney too. If somehow we get separated, he says I am to go straight to the Sebel Townhouse near Kings Cross. He will take the hash from me there, and then I can go to Byron Bay to be with the children while he continues on to Melbourne.

We return to our seats, and within half an hour we are descending into Sydney.

Eddie needs to arrange for his luggage to be taken off in Sydney, so I pass through Immigration alone. But as I am shepherded towards the baggage collection area, it hits me: what am I trying to do here? The Valium is still heavy in my limbs but suddenly I feel awake. I can't do this. I still have to pass through Customs. I start to freak out.

I spot Eddie near the carousel and I can't get to him fast enough. I'm sick, I tell him. This is horrible. I want to get rid of it. I just want to go to the bathroom and throw the stuff away.

Come on, Donna, we're nearly there, he says. Not long to go now. Just stay calm.

My head is throbbing, Eddie can't find his luggage, and now he is walking away from me, telling me to join the Customs queue, he'll meet me there in a minute.

I head over to the queue but it is moving too quickly and before I know it, I find myself going through Customs alone. I can't shake this strange feeling.

I hand the Customs officer my handbag and he opens it up. Sitting on top, in full view, is a small brown packet that I don't recognise. The Customs officer pulls it out.

What is this? he asks.

I don't know, I say (and I don't).

I look around for Eddie but he is nowhere to be seen.

CHAPTER 18

The small brown packet is now lying in the palm of the Customs officer's hand. He slowly opens it to reveal what he later refers to as 'green vegetable matter'. He calls over one of his colleagues and then everything goes mad. They know. They are going through my things, they have found the hash. More officers are called over and they are taking me away to be searched.

Who are you travelling with? one asks.

Oh God.

I'm travelling on my own.

A couple of Customs officers take me into an interview room. There is just a desk and a couple of chairs. I try to think back to the plane: where did that little brown packet come from? It wasn't with the other stuff Eddie gave me. Even if it had been, I certainly wouldn't have left anything sitting right at the top of my handbag. The bag was lying open under the seat in front of me on the plane. Someone must have put it in then. Only I didn't see it when I pulled my passport out to go through Immigration.

One of the Customs officers hands me a card. Read this, please.

I look down at the title: *Search of Persons, Section 196, Customs Act*. I am struck by how official it is.

The Customs officer gives me a couple of minutes then asks, Have you read and understood the card?

Yes.

Do you have any objections to being body-searched?

No.

The Customs officers leave and are replaced by two police-women. The one who seems to be in charge notes the time – it is 9.10 am – and introduces herself.

I am Detective Constable Thompson. I am from the Australian Federal Police drug unit and this is Detective Watts.

This is way too real.

Donna, you are not obliged to say anything unless you wish to do so, as anything you do say will be taken down and later be given in evidence. Do you understand that?

Yes.

Detective Thompson starts documenting the packages of hash, while her colleague photographs it all. Everything is on full show. I am a criminal.

What do these packages contain? Detective Thompson asks.

Hash. It's all hash.

Once she has finished recording the drugs, she asks, Do you have any other narcotics secreted about your body?

No, what do you mean?

Do you have any narcotics or anything secreted in your vagina?

No.

The one doing all the talking leaves the room. My head is spinning. *What have I done? What have I done?* The policewoman returns with a male officer.

Donna, this is Detective Constable Johnson and he is also

from the Australian Federal Police drug unit. He has some questions he would like to ask you.

He reads me my rights and asks where I have come from this morning.

Bombay.

Were you travelling with anyone?

Shit. No.

Do you know a person called Edward Myatt?

Shit, shit. Yes.

Were you travelling with him?

No. (I am really panicking now, but all I can think is that there is no point in both of us going down. I need Eddie free so he can help to get me out of here.)

Was he on the same flight as you?

Yes.

What is your relationship with Edward Myatt?

We used to live together.

Did you leave Australia together?

Yes.

Did you sit with Edward on your return flight?

I sat near him.

Did you speak to Edward in the Customs Hall?

Yes, but we had an argument and he didn't want to talk to me and I walked away from him.

What was the argument about?

We had split up in India and he was with others over there.

Does Edward know about the hashish?

No, he would kill me if he knew.

What the hell am I saying here? I don't know what I am bloody meant to say. How could I be so stupid? Eddie, I need you. Please get help, please please please.

The policeman is continuing with his questions. Where did you get the hashish?

India.

When did you get the hash?

I don't want to say.

The questions pour heavy from his mouth, burying me.

Look, I finally say, I don't want to say anything about it. Edward doesn't know about this . . . I want to go to the toilet.

It turns out they have arrested Eddie, too. Obviously, they can see that we bought our airline tickets together on my credit card, so they bring him in. He is taken to another room and searched but he is clean as a whistle – externally. And I suppose because I have said he has nothing to do with it, they let him go. So he goes to a hotel in Bondi and I go to Federal Police headquarters.

It is late morning by the time the two female officers and I arrive there. They take me to another interview room for more questioning and tell me that I am facing up to twenty-five years in jail and/or a $100,000 fine – unless I can convince the court that I wasn't planning to make money out of the hash, in which case I would still be facing two years in jail or a $2000 fine.

They want to make a deal, they say. Why don't I talk to them. Why don't I tell them where I got the hash, who else is involved? But I don't know. I don't know anything.

The policewomen are setting up a tape recorder, getting out their pens and paper. But I have decided the best thing to do is just keep my mouth shut from now on.

The one in charge is speaking again: What I now intend to do is to conduct a record of interview with you . . . Do you under-stand that?

Yes, but I won't sign anything.

Are you prepared to take part in a record of interview?

No.

Are you prepared to read the notes of your earlier conversations with Detective Johnson and myself?

No.

Would you be prepared to sign the notes?

No.

I inform you formally that you are under arrest for the importation and possession of cannabis resin. You will shortly be taken to the Sydney Police Centre, where you will be charged with those offences. Do you understand that?

Yes . . . Will I get out today or will I go to jail?

That will be up to the magistrate.

I am charged and taken to the Sydney Watch House for the night. I have a court appearance in the morning and if I get bail, I can go home. If I don't, I will go to jail.

I get hold of the well-known Sydney criminal lawyer Chris Murphy and in the morning, someone from his office turns up to represent me at court. It is the Christmas holidays and the magistrates are off work; Justices of the Peace are presiding in their place. My lawyer advises me to ask for my case to be adjourned rather than apply for bail as a JP is almost certain to refuse it. He says that once bail is refused it is nearly impossible to overturn. He says I am better off spending a week in jail on remand, and then going before a magistrate to apply for bail when they get back from holidays.

I am in shock at this stage. Everything is a fog. So I go along with the lawyer's advice.

As we are sitting in court awaiting my turn, the woman in front of me, represented by Legal Aid, is granted $5000 bail for importing pure heroin. I can't help wondering why I wouldn't be granted bail for the lesser crime of importing hashish.

Especially considering that I have no prior criminal record. But my lawyer does not apply.

So I spend a second night at the Watch House and at 9.30 the next morning they drive me to Mulawa Women's Detention Centre at Silverwater. Jail. I am going to jail. It is Christmas Eve.

I stumble through the admissions process of questions and forms and tests.

Medical history?

Bowel problems, hypotension, dizziness.

Psychiatric history?

None.

Gynaecological?

Period pain.

Last menstrual period?

Last month.

Could you be pregnant?

No. The doctor told me I can't have any more children.

They give me one of those urine pregnancy tests anyway, and it is negative.

No, I didn't think so.

The questions continue. Did I wag school a lot? Did I go to lots of schools? Any drug abuse? No, no, no. Alcohol abuse? Only socially.

Weight?

Seven stone.

Height?

Five foot three.

They record in my notes that I am tearful.

They ask me if I want to have an AIDS test, a hepatitis test. I think they think I am a drug addict because I am pretty thin. No thanks.

I vaguely remember them searching me, checking me in. I am in shock. Then I go into the jail.

They put me in a cell on my own. An observation cell, they call it. It has just a bed and a shitty old toilet that may well never have been cleaned. It is beyond imagining and I begin to freak out. I know I am in real trouble. One moment of madness, and look where I am. My whole future is gone. That is all I keep thinking. I cannot believe I have given up everything I have worked so hard for, for myself and my kids. I am back where I started: locked up with all the other naughty girls, in just another orphanage. And this time it is my own fault. The weird thing is that I have always had a fear I was going to end up locked up again. So, in some ways, I actually feel a bit secure. A bit relieved. I don't have to worry now, because this is where I belong. Someone will bring me my food, someone will tell me when to sleep, what to do. I can be a little girl again. I don't have to deal with life. Being alone in an orphanage and running away and hiding sometimes is okay. This is home to me. But at the same time I know you can't run away from here. Not like the orphanage or even Winlaton.

So, despite the eerie sense of security, I cannot stop crying. I can't sleep.

The guards come round every hour to offer cigarettes. I don't smoke so I always say no. But then a girl comes up to me through the bars and says, You do smoke. You take your smokes, and you give them to me. I have to let the guards light it for me, but then I stub it out and hand it over to her.

I get steadily more depressed. I don't know how I can survive this. Jesus Christ, what a bloody idiot I am. It makes me feel sick to think about it. How could I have been so weak? I am sobbing, feeling like I'm losing my mind. I am definitely not going to last the distance.

Eddie comes to visit. Thank goodness I have Eddie. He has stuck by me. I am so embarrassed by what I have done I don't want him to tell anyone, but he brings along some old friends of mine, Pam and Barry. They cannot believe that I have broken the law – smuggling drugs, especially. But Pam is wonderful. Don't worry, we'll get bail and we'll get you out.

And Eddie is doing everything he can to help. He comes back two or three times during the week. He is with me every step of the way. I'm going to get you out of here, I promise you. Don't worry, sweetheart, we'll be together soon.

Xmas 89
Jessie darling, as you would have realised I wasn't around for Xmas. Our first Xmas apart. I was detained for a while. I will explain everything whenever you ask. Hope you had a beautiful Xmas and I'm sorry I didn't call you. I feel such pain, I can't begin to tell you. I want to see the sunlight, the trees, the birds and walk on the grass, I don't want to be locked up in this awful cell. I can't sleep, I'm hungry, I can't eat without feeling sick. I clean my teeth and I feel sick. I ask for food at odd times, I'm refused as it's against regulations. It's my own fault. Xmas eve.

Thank you Pam, Barry and Ed for coming to see me, for being my true friends . . .

I put on a brave face but after they left I felt so lonely, sad & scared. It brings back my awful childhood & I don't & can't stand the pain.

. . . Poor Ed! I wonder what he'll do, if he'll stand by me. So far everything seems OK.

On Boxing Day they move me from the observation cell to a

159

dormitory. Rows of beds, bars on the windows. I really am back in the orphanage now. Just a number. No escape.

There are maybe ten girls in here. All on remand. One tells me: Watch y'self, cos I'm a killer. She murdered a girlfriend or something. Then, in the middle of the night, one gets out of bed and bashes up another girl. It is clear that this place thrives on fear. The only way I can cope is to believe I will make bail and get out.

I have my wedding ring, which the guards have let me keep, and some of the girls want to take it from me. Have it as a souvenir. I tell them that I won't give it to them but they say, Oh yes you will. So I say, All right, I'll give it to you when my bail comes through.

You won't get bail.

This is becoming more than I can handle. I might have made it through my upbringing by developing strong survival skills but even they are not enough here; I am out of my depth. It is like the walls are closing in on me. The girls are going to get me. And I am sick. Every time I put anything in my mouth I want to vomit. The guards write in my file that I am not coping.

Pam comes back to visit with the news that bail has been set at $65,000 dollars. I will be released when I can raise the money. It is a lot of bail for a first offence. Especially considering that girl I saw in court who was charged with importing heroin got out on $5000 bail. I sack my lawyer.

In jail, a lot of the girls can't even raise $1000 bail, so when I go back to the dormitory saying bail has been set at $65,000, some of them tell me, You won't raise that. You'll be around for a while, love.

I'll get the money.

Yeah, yeah, that's what they all say.

Every minute I am in this place is suffocating. It is like the girls are closing in on me. At last I can see the guard calling my name. Donna Ehrenburg, your bail's come through. Only the girls are trying to trap me in here. They are going to cause a fight. All I am thinking is, Get those gates open, get those gates open and let me out. I pretend to take off my wedding ring, as if I am going to give it to someone. And the gates are opening, and as soon as I have the all clear, I bolt. I am escaping all over again.

CHAPTER 19

Eddie is waiting out the front for me. I am so glad to see him. I have spent six nights in custody, four of them in jail. I am feeling sick and I know I am in really bad trouble. All I want is some-one's arms around me.

Eddie takes me back to his hotel but when I get into bed with him, he goes cold. I assumed we were back together, but now he has a confused look on his face and he is saying, I want my space, I want my space.

2nd Jan 1990
I've just spent one week in jail, Eddie seeing me at every opportunity telling me he loves me & can't wait to get me out of this awful place then I get out, the night was good, but then the next morning I realised it wasn't a nightmare. I'm confused & thinking about the whole time I was on the plane coming home. I'm crying freaked out so sad scared & all Eddie could say was don't cling to me, I want my space. He wants to go to Melbourne alone.

I went outside. If a car had hit me I would
welcome it.

Jan 4th 90
On the train going home to Byron, impossible to
sleep, my mind is a mass of words, so much chatter going on in my head. I feel scared, lonely,
I miss Jessie & poor Dylan . . .
My time in jail was only 1 week although it
seemed like eternity. It brought back all that
orphanage confusion. The nuns were so cruel to
girls, why I'll never know, they had no understanding, we were there for some crime our
mothers did, we were innocent, it was the sad-
dest time of my life. And now again.

I return to Byron Bay a criminal. I have to report to the police
three times a week and the court has frozen all my assets. They
must think I am some big-time drug dealer. The court order
prevents me disposing of any property, only giving me some
pocket money to meet 'reasonable living expenses'. If I want to
spend anything more, I have to seek approval from the Director
of Public Prosecutions.

The police return my belongings, but my perfume and other
bits and pieces have disappeared from my luggage. Christmas
presents I bought overseas for the kids are gone. At least my
journal is intact. It is no longer reading material for Jessie and
Dylan, though. Now it is my outlet for all the craziness swirling
through my head. I wish I could confide in a person, rather than
this diary, but how do I explain my stupidity? There are not
words to fix what I have done.

I feel so bad arriving home, because word spreads around
town. The chamber magistrate, who enlisted my support to

campaign for a new courthouse, finds out. It is humiliating. And no one can believe it; it is so unlike me, I am someone who didn't need to do this, I had money. But for me it was never about money, it was an emotional thing. I can't explain that to anyone. It sounds like excuses, which I suppose it is. There is no excuse; I bloody did this. I brought the drugs in. I just want to hide.

I wish that my kids were here but how could I let them see me day in and day out depressed and crying, not knowing what to do? I feel so bad for them, especially Jessie. Dylan has always been independent, whereas Jessie is one of those children who never lets go of your apron strings. Wherever I go, she has a grip on my dress and her thumb in her mouth. At least by leaving her with Robert, if I end up going to jail she will already be settled. Robert is living up in Toowoomba, a hundred kilometres west of Brisbane, so it is close enough for the children to visit me at weekends. I explain to them as best I can what is going on. I tell them that I have done something very wrong and that I will have to accept my punishment, but that it doesn't mean they have done anything wrong or that I love them any less. They know there is a chance I could go to jail. I feel I have to prepare them for the worst, and I would rather they hear it from me than from anyone else. In some ways, they are being stronger about it than I am.

Eddie arrives in Byron Bay and stays in the house with me, but nothing has changed since India. He won't make love with me anymore. We continue to play our game of cat and mouse. Most of the time it feels like he can't stand me, but then I distance myself and he is all loving again.

I get a phone call from the Byron Bay cops: How about meeting with us? You just name the date. Anytime, anywhere.

Why? I ask.

We just want to talk to you. You might be able to help us, we might be able to help you.

So I phone my lawyer and ask, Could the Byron Bay police help me? And he wants to know, Are they harassing you?

I don't know if you would call it harassment but I am curious to find out why they want to meet me.

The lawyer tells me to keep right away from them. Then he rings the Byron Bay police station and says, Don't harass my client.

They probably think I am a big-time dealer too. They are probably hoping to crack a major syndicate or something.

I return to Sydney for a bail continuance hearing, and then Eddie wants to go to Melbourne to see his family so I join him.

I am still sick all the time, vomiting and tired. I assume it is stress, but just in case I picked up something in India, while I am in Melbourne I phone a friend who is a doctor. He owns a diagnostic clinic and tells me to come in the following weekend so he can check me out.

I meet him on the Saturday and he decides to do an ultrasound on my tummy to try to figure out what is making me so unwell. He squeezes the tube of gel onto my belly and is having a look when suddenly he says, Oh my goodness, you're pregnant. You are about fourteen weeks pregnant.

It's not possible, I can't be pregnant, it's not possible. But I can see the little hands and button nose on the screen. The heart beating. I am having a baby.

He tells me I am due in August. I figure out I must have been about six weeks along when I was arrested. The urine test they gave me in jail must have shown a false negative. All that time in India that I was feeling sick and emotional I was actually pregnant. At the ashram, on the plane home . . .

I head over to Eddie's sister's house. Eddie is there, along with his mother, May. And I say, I've got some news. I'm having a baby. You are going to be a grandmother, you're going to be an aunty, and Eddie, you are going to be a daddy.

They go dead quiet. The colour drains from Eddie's face.

He and I walk down the street. Get rid of it, he says.

I say, I don't think I can get rid of it because I've already seen it. I want to keep it.

Already I am attached to this budding little person. I had assumed I would never have another child; now I have been given a second chance. Why has this happened now? I think of the babies I have lost and can't help wondering whether this one will make it to full term. I don't know if I could cope with the loss of another child. I am scared.

Having a baby changes my priorities. I ask Eddie to see a marriage counsellor with me; trying to work out what to do, I am grasping at straws but I need to offer this child the best I can. He or she is going to need as much love as I can give. Eddie is not keen on counselling but agrees to go twice. During our second session he takes me by surprise when he opens up about India and the hash; how sorry he feels that I got busted when I was only doing it for him. It is the first time he has admitted his involvement to someone else. It is such a relief to hear him shoulder some of the blame that for a moment I feel like everything is going to be okay. The police will see that I am not a big-time drug dealer, Eddie will confess and I will be free to go home and look after my children.

Afterwards, I ask Eddie if he plans to go to the cops and tell them what he told the counsellor.

I'll think about it, he says.

Eddie, please, you have to go to the police and tell them the truth.

Yeah, all right, mate, all right.

It is then that I realise the seriousness of Eddie's game-playing. He doesn't want the baby, and yet he is still living with

166

me. He hates me one minute and loves me the next. There is a part of me that has a deep attachment to him, but another part is asking a lot of questions. I am beginning to wonder why Eddie gave me the Valium on the plane. Was it him who put the drugs in my bag? Maybe he used me as a decoy so he could get his other stuff through. Would he do that to me? He knows me well enough to know that my early life was difficult, I am vulnerable, I am loyal. If only I'd had more time to think about it, been a bit clearer in my head – Jesus Christ, what an idiot I was to weaken and bring in the hash. Something happened to me emotionally that made me do it. I was thirty-nine and had a handsome young boyfriend who was slipping away. I just wanted him to love me. That is all I can think of to justify what I did. I need to understand it myself. But even if I could understand it, deep in my heart I know there is really no justification for it. I did this. I have to take responsibility.

More importantly, though, I now have to protect my child. I do not want my baby to be born in jail and taken away from me, as I was taken from my mother.

If Eddie really loves me, he will go to the police and tell them the truth.

```
Feb 27 '90
I haven't been able to write for a while, too dis-
tressed. Eddie don't read my diary. I wonder how
Jessie will cope when I tell her about the baby.
I love you Jessie and hope you can love the baby
too. Don't really know what to do anymore . . .
```

```
Byron 3rd March
Jessie & Dylan here for the weekend, how nice
it is to see their faces, spend time with them,
how precious time with them is, now I'm facing
```

jail. I feel for you Jessie & I'm sorry, I'm so
glad you both are happy about the baby . . .

Please, if fate is with me . . . don't let this
babe be born under police protection. Not in
jail. I just couldn't cope. I want the baby born
in this house, Old Bangalow Rd, Jessie & Dylan
& maybe Eddie at my side. I want it to be a perfect birth . . .

Go to the police, Ed.

6th March
I fear I may have a breakdown if this nightmare
doesn't stop.

4am just can't sleep. Maybe dying is my only
way out.

I sit on my verandah alone and wonder what it is like to die. To
finally let go. It would be an amazing feeling, to give up the
fight. I think about that a lot now. This nightmare has been
going on since December, every day consumed by my awful
mistake.

Eddie still hasn't gone to the police, so I phone my lawyer and
tell him how Eddie admitted everything to our marriage counsellor and ask if there is any way we could use this. Could we
subpoena the counsellor's files? But the lawyer says No, sorry
Donna, it's all confidential.

I don't know what I expected, really. I had thought Eddie
would bend over backwards to help me.

I decide to go and see Eddie's ex-wife, Annsilvana. I am getting
desperate. So I turn up at her little flat in Bondi. She is a tall, thin,
black woman, very beautiful but overly made-up so she looks a bit
like a transvestite. She is a sannyasin and runs a business called
Private Passions, selling beautiful mosquito nets and exotic lingerie.

She is very open with me. I tell her about my getting busted bringing hash in from India and she is not at all surprised. She and Eddie also travelled in India and he packed her bags to come home. She didn't know until much later that he had put hash in her bag, and, luckily for her, Customs didn't know either. He did that to her twice, she says. She left him after that.

Speaking with Annsilvana makes me realise how Eddie uses women. I feel so stupid for allowing myself to be sucked in by him. I just want to go back to the way things were before I met him. I want my children back with me, I want to give birth to my baby in peace and to continue on with my life. I never had a family when I was little; I don't want to lose the one that I have now. I do not want my children to lose their mother.

The doctor says I am not eating well enough. I am anaemic and a bit underweight. So late in March he sends me to Byron Bay Hospital for some bed rest. This pregnancy is a small miracle as it is, and I think the doctor is worried that I won't make it to term. This stage of pregnancy is the start of the danger zone for someone like me with an incompetent cervix. After what my womb has been through and the way I haemorrhaged last time, the doctor isn't taking any chances. I think he can also see that I am having an emotional breakdown.

I am discharged from hospital a week later, still in pain physically and emotionally, but at least the doctors tell me the baby is okay. Against the odds, this little one is hanging in there. I try to be strong for my baby but I feel the light slipping away every day. It is as though Donna doesn't exist anymore. The baby doesn't get any emotional nourishment from me and I feel helpless.

Mostly I just feel alone. Eddie is hardly ever around anymore. He visited me once while I was in hospital but I felt nothing. I only wish now I had told the truth in the first place. I could have spared myself all the pain. The lawyers, too, are advising me that it is time to come clean. I think they can see that my attachment to Eddie is increasingly tenuous and they say the truth is my only chance.

I am such an emotional wreck that instead of thinking it through, I go to Eddie in a fit of anger and tell him I can't, I won't, protect him anymore. I have given him every opportunity to go to the police himself and tell them exactly what happened. Even though, yes, I did bring the hash in, there was a lot more to it than that.

I plead with him. You are on your own, you'll get a couple of years in jail, you will do it and then you'll get out. Please, just come clean. I've got three people depending on me. My children and this unborn child.

If he does not come clean soon, I am going to tell the police myself. I need to protect my baby. I will not allow us to be separated.

2nd April
I must accept I am alone in all of this, as I was in the orphanage. My way of handling it was to cut off my emotions then & I did it so well. People out there are all so cruel: lawyers, police, judges, lovers. I now want to cut off from them all. Be strong.

3rd April
I must start to become very positive. I am going to believe the judge will be compassionate towards me & allow my baby to be born where I choose & also not separate baby & me . . .

8th April
Starting to feel good about having a baby. From the beginning I want to do everything right. Ideal birth, would very much like to have a water birth. I believe the child has gone through so much trauma in my womb. I must fix all that now. This child deserves love & will get it, I promise you that . . .

10th April
I ask Ed to be with me at the birth, get me through the final stages of my pregnancy. Ed answers, I might if you give me the car back. Why has my fate chosen him as the father of my child? Does his cruelty end? I do wish he would leave town, a man with no compassion. I'm sorry, little one inside my womb.

Eddie disappears. Someone tells me he is living with an artist, another older woman with a house near the beach. So I go around to see her. I am about five months pregnant by now. I say to her, So it looks like Eddie's hanging out with you now.

And she says, Oh, he's such a spiritual man, isn't he.

I just look at her and think, You idiot. You know damn well Eddie is a drug dealer. Don't hide him in your house. I am carrying his child, for heaven's sake.

I even phone Eddie's sister down in Melbourne: You know what your brother's like, and you would still let a pregnant woman go to jail for him?

I can't believe he can do this. I am literally left holding the baby.

Anyway, they obviously tell Eddie about my explosions of

anger and he can see I am becoming unbalanced. So he makes himself scarce.

That's when I finally phone Detective Constable Thompson at the Federal Police: I really need to talk to you. It's time to put my cards on the table.

Over the phone I tell her the basics: how Eddie had a bellyful when he went through Customs; how he bought it all and planned to sell it. They already suspect him anyway, with his connection to the sannyasins and all his overseas trips. I tell her Eddie could be staying at the Suffolk Park Caravan Park in Byron Bay and volunteer to be wired up to try to get him on tape discussing his involvement. I then arrange to make a formal statement the following week when I am in Sydney for a court appearance.

17th April
Going to Sydney, Eddie nowhere to be found, driving down alone. I really believed he would come to my rescue & take me. He knows I'm $5\frac{1}{2}$ mths pregnant & the pain I've been in . . . He leaves me no choice with what I have to do.

CHAPTER 20

I meet with the Federal Police in Sydney to make my statement. It is a relief to get it all out finally. I tell them everything, from when Eddie first came into my life, to the gold we bought and took to India, and Eddie's decision to bring hash back to Australia. I tell them how when they first interviewed me I was protecting Eddie, and continued to do so because I was waiting for him to prove his love and go to the authorities with the truth.

And, of course, I tell them how I have since discovered that I am pregnant; how it partly explains why I was so ill and emotional in India. I can sense the police softening towards me. I get the feeling they are starting to realise that they've got the wrong person.

I sign the statement thinking, At last, I don't have to worry about this attachment to Eddie anymore. He is obviously not going to take care of things, so now the police can take charge.

It turns out to be a waste of time. By the time the police go up to Byron to arrest Eddie, he has shot through. Their searches reveal he left the country sometime between me making my phone call to the Feds and making my statement in Sydney. When I hear that, I feel numb, then sick. I just cry and cry. I can't believe he would desert me that way.

At the same time, it now all makes sense. While I thought he was sticking around to help me with the case, all he wanted to do was get his car and go. I only bought the car from him because he told me it had been in the family for twenty years and he would be devastated to part with it. How gullible am I? Now his sister tells me it wasn't a family car at all. And yet he had the nerve to stick around purely so he could get it back.

What sort of a man are you, Eddie? How could you do this to another human being? What am I supposed to tell your child about you?

Eddie taking off turns out to be especially bad for me because now the cops think I might actually have helped him escape. Never mind that I was cooperating with police in order to catch him, and that I didn't even know he had left the country. Besides, I ask them, how come he was allowed to fly out in the first place? I had already told the detective over the phone about his involvement so why wasn't there some sort of alert out for him? Eddie must have nerves of steel, to go to an airport and leave the country when he knew I was planning to go to the police about him. I suppose he has to if he is going to make his living swallowing drugs – walk through the airport cool as a cucumber, crap them out, clean them off and sell them. How could you live your life like that?

Eddie doesn't return to Australia, but he sends me a letter explaining his disappearing act. It is postmarked Sydney, 1 May, and yet the Feds say he left on 16 April. It doesn't make sense. The letter is typical Eddie: he had no choice but to leave and he knows that I can handle this much better than he could because I am the strong one. Blah blah blah.

He phones once or twice too. I don't really know what he wants. He comes over all loving and spiritual but he is angry because I have sold his car. He can't see the bigger picture; that I may go to jail, I may lose my baby. All my assets are frozen, the lawyers are milking me dry, I haven't got my children with me.

I'll give you karma, Eddie.

Still in Sydney, I have an ultrasound and see an obstetrician. All this stress can't be good for my little one. But the doctors put my mind at rest; they tell me the baby is fine, and that he is a boy. A beautiful little boy. I watch him floating on the screen even though I am too scared to love him. Dear God, please don't send me to jail. Who will look after my baby?

The doctor tells me I have a low-lying placenta, which means I will need to have another ultrasound later in the pregnancy. He is also worried that I am too thin. I need to eat more and stop worrying so much.

Tell me how. I have so many court appearances, back and forth from Sydney to Byron Bay. It is still another month before D-day, when I enter my plea, but in the meantime we are preoccupied with trying to get the Director of Public Prosecutions to release my assets. The lawyers are especially keen on this because once I have access to my money I can pay their bill. More importantly, as far as I am concerned, if the DPP releases my assets it will mean they have given me the all clear. They will have investigated where every cent has come from and essentially they will be saying, Yes, that all makes sense, it is all accounted for. Which will be good when we go to court because we can say, See, none of my money has come from drug dealing. I think the police are still worried that I am a big-time dealer.

Anyway, it is very easy for me to explain where my assets have come from because it pretty much boils down to real estate: I bought this house for this much, sold it for that much. And I have paid all my taxes over the years. We have given the DPP all that information, so it will just be a matter of time before they release everything. But I am starting to learn that with the legal system, nothing happens quickly. Each time we go to court the matter is adjourned, and every time a court matter is adjourned the lawyers are making more money from me. Ching-ching. I am so cash-strapped I have to go on the pension. It is not just the legal fees – it is the airfares. I am sick, I am pregnant.

The lawyers don't see how hard this is for me. To them it is just a job. For example, they keep telling me, Get your kids back, get your kids back. Have your kids living with you, it will be much better for the sentencing.

I desperately want my kids back but what about their stability? How can I disrupt them like that when I may be going to jail in a month or two? I can't do it.

I so much want to be happy but the walls are collapsing around me.

I turn to a fresh page in my journal and write my will. Maybe I am so sad I will just die in my sleep. In the morning, things seem a little better. They always do.

Over the next few days I have appointments with two psychiatrists. The lawyers need one of them to give evidence in court as to my state of mind, but I also need to see them for myself. I need to work out why I did what I did. How did I get to the point I had survived living in an orphanage, I had made something of my life – a few bumps and wrong turns, but nevertheless – I had two beautiful children, and then I allowed this to happen? That is why I am so traumatised now. Things were good and I destroyed it all.

I visit the well-known psychiatrist Robert Hampshire in his Macquarie Street office. I tell him I want to know why I allowed a man to convince me to bring two kilos of hash into the country. I see Dr Hampshire a number of times. We talk about my childhood and my relationship with men. I can be so tough and so self-sufficient, but where men are concerned, I become vulnerable. Something weird happens to me. What is it? Dr Hampshire says I have post-traumatic shock from my childhood and that I hold men responsible for protecting me from that. He turns out to be a great support for me over the coming months.

The other psychiatrist I see is called William Barclay. He is very good, too. He recognises that I didn't bring the drugs in for monetary gain, that it was purely an emotional thing that I did for Eddie. He says my upbringing in institutions meant there was an absence of bonding with others, and so ever since then I have been looking to be loved. He says that is why I leap into relationships, mostly without any judgement, and then often the relationships turn out to be disasters. Dr Barclay thinks that, just as I fantasised about an imaginary family when I was younger, I make believe that I am deeply in love and that these relationships have more promise than they really do. Anyway, that is his understanding of how I could have done something so stupid for a man.

Bringing all the orphanage stuff up again is traumatic. I have tried all these years to detach myself from the pain; it is more than I can handle. I leave one of my appointments feeling so raw I almost walk in front of a truck. I want the truck to hit me. I am crying, lost . . . But I can't – my children.

28.4.90
 . . . I'm in a pond, I'm sinking & I don't know
how to get out.

CHAPTER 21

4.5.90
Today I fell in love with my babe. It's not
Eddie's babe, it is mine. I felt the urge to go
buy baby clothes but I can't because it's a bad
omen. I will wait till the court case is over
& I don't go to jail. Who can I give my babe to
if it happens? Eddie's gone.

6th May
Back home from Syd. It feels good to be back
home at Old Bangalow Rd. I do like it here . . .
    Ed, you don't know what you're missing out
on. I'm just now looking down at my belly, looking at the babe kicking away. It's so amazing
to watch something moving around inside of me.

My lawyer tells me my case is looking good and that I am not
going to jail. He is so confident that for a brief moment I laugh
and let myself imagine that everything is going to turn out okay;
I will return home to my family and give birth to my baby free

and in peace. But then I stop myself. I am not going to get carried away just yet.

D-day is a little over a week away and as it draws nearer, my moods spin ever more out of control: my depressions send me to a black place I sometimes think I will never crawl out of. But then I remember the little life growing inside me and I know I have to find the light. If I go down, so does my baby.

I concentrate my energies on my case. On Monday I am due in court to appear before Judge Solomon and plead guilty, and the following Thursday we are back in court for my sentencing hearing.

I have chosen to plead guilty with mitigating circumstances, and to allow the Crown to question me. My lawyers think this should help in making the judge give me a lighter punishment – hopefully a fine rather than a jail sentence. You can plead guilty and say nothing, but I have agreed to tell them whatever they want to know. The fact that I am pleading guilty should also stand in my favour.

At the sentencing hearing, it is our job to convince the judge that even though I did this, I do not deserve to go to jail for it. It is unnerving that my life is in this judge's hands. He doesn't know me, he doesn't know my children – how could I have got myself into a situation where a complete stranger will decide my fate?

At the sentencing hearing I will be the first defence witness to take the stand, so, in preparation, my barrister puts me through hour upon hour of questioning. She attacks me, trips me up, harangues me, until I feel utterly wrung-out and my belly begins to ache.

Nevertheless, I feel ready and things are looking positive. My friend David Hanlon, a lawyer from Melbourne, comes up to help with my case, and the chamber magistrate from Byron Bay – the one I campaigned with for the new courthouse – writes a letter of support to the judge. There are other character witnesses too. I just have to pray that the judge will let me go home – and that he makes his decision as quickly as possible. There is a chance he could hand down his sentence on the day but it could also be weeks, or even months, that this drags on. I just want the whole thing to be over with.

Jessie and Dylan come down to stay with me for the weekend. I pray it is not my last weekend with them. I do not tell them that I have my sentencing hearing this week, that I could go straight to jail. They know it is a possibility somewhere down the line, but I just cannot bring myself to say the words. As far as they know, I am going down to Sydney for another minor court date. I am all smiles.

But really, I am barely able to cope. I have to prepare for the worst. I wake at 4 am and can't get back to sleep. I am so tired, between the baby and the stress, but I keep thinking, *This may be my last weekend here. I may not see my kids grow up.* I don't know what to do with the house; I start to pack but then I just cry. I don't know where to begin. There is so much to do and the weekend is running out, my time unravelling.

Suddenly, it is Sunday afternoon. I am sitting on the verandah, Jessie tucked in next to me, waiting for my lift to the airport. I still haven't told the kids it may be a long time before I return. I can't.

It is a strange feeling getting off the plane in Sydney, with no one to meet me, no one to carry my bag, nearly seven months pregnant and facing jail.

On Monday morning I head to the Supreme Court feeling surprisingly strong – only tired – ready to enter my guilty plea.

I almost have a sense of relief because it is a step closer to the end.

I sit in the coffee shop for two hours waiting to meet my lawyer, Paul. He is supposed to pick me up at noon, in time to accompany me to court, but the appointed hour comes and goes and he is nowhere to be seen. I can feel myself becoming anxious. My strength is draining away. Eventually I give up and walk to the courtroom by myself.

I find my barrister, Elizabeth Fullerton, there in the foyer. She looks up at me and yells: Where's Paul?

Who knows?

She tells me that, with no sign of Paul or me, she was forced to face court without us and wear the consequences.

Well, we've lost Judge Solomon, she spits. Now we've got Judge Knoblanche and he is tough.

Elizabeth walks out, leaving me standing there all alone. Tears just seem to stream down my face. God, I have had enough of lawyers. The first thing they learn in law school must be, Don't get too close. The client is just a number. Bloody hell, woman, I could go to jail and lose my baby.

It is left to the DPP's Liz Ryan – the one prosecuting me, for goodness sake – to console me. You will be okay, she says.

I tell her I am not a drug dealer, I have just made a terrible mistake.

I can see her compassion as she says, I'm not allowed to talk to you, Donna.

22nd May
Two days to go, the diarrhoea is getting worse.
I called David Reid [doctor], he said it's fear
& wished me good luck . . .

5am 23rd
D-day tomorrow. Judge Knoblanche, give me my
freedom.

5am D-day 24th May
I don't know what to do next. I have no faith
in Paul, he wants another $2000. I haven't got
it. Once again I have to borrow it. I've bor-
rowed so much money from so many people, my
assets are still frozen, what will I do. I suppose after today if I go to jail I won't be able
to write anymore. I remember from when I was
there at Xmas I wasn't allowed to have my diary.

Dear Jessie,
    Spending last weekend with you was the great-
est moment for me. I just couldn't bring it upon
myself to tell you I may [not see you for a long
time], my darling I'm so sorry for letting you
down. If I could undo it all I would . . .
    I hope I have loved you enough throughout the
years my darling & you don't make terrible mis-
takes as I have made. Don't ever forget Jess I
love you & I cry as I write this because sorry
I may not see you grow up. God please Judge
Knoblanche think of my children. I am not a bad
person, Jessie is so dependent upon me. When I
told her a couple of months ago what lay ahead
her answer was, Mum they won't put you in jail,
the judge is a good man, he won't take you away
from me & my brother or sister, he just wouldn't
do it. Jessie I hope you are right. Until I see
you again I love you.

Dear Dylan,

You are now 15 years old darling & will have to grow up fast if I go to jail. I wanted to talk to you about it before but I just couldn't. I wanted to spare you the pain, just in case I got my freedom. You are a good boy darling & if we have had any differences in the past I suppose it's all a part of you growing up & me getting to know you. Just remember Dylan whilst you were growing up I gave you all the love I could as I know what it's like to not be loved as a child. I hope with whatever happens to me it doesn't affect you in a negative way & I'm sorry for not being more mature & for being so stupid. I hope you can love your little brother darling, he's going to need all the love he can find after everything that has happened to him in the womb. I wanted to tell you it may be my last weekend with you but I just couldn't. Farewell to you, what a strange feeling of emptiness, I felt so lonely. Love you. Mumma

CHAPTER 22

8.30 am D-day.

I drive to the airport to pick up my lawyer friend, David Hanlon, who has flown in from Melbourne, and we head straight to a meeting with Elizabeth Fullerton. She wants a conference with David before we are due in court this morning.

On our way up to Elizabeth's twelfth-floor office, the elevator jolts to a halt, mid-floor. Suddenly we aren't moving anymore, and it takes me a few seconds to realise: we are trapped. Of all the things to happen on this day . . .

I am frightened just to be stuck in this cramped, airless space, but to be stuck here pregnant and now running late for court is almost unbearable. My chest tightens. Every precious minute seems to drag into eternity as the prospect of missing my own sentencing hearing becomes a reality. Why aren't we moving? Where is everybody? Why aren't we being rescued?

We are in there for close to an hour by the time we are released. Long enough to mean we have missed our appearance. Consequently, we end up losing Judge Knoblanche, the supposedly tough judge, and I am reassigned to appear before Judge David Shillington.

I arrive to see Judge Shillington winding up the sentencing on another case, so I sit in and watch to get an idea of what sort of a judge he is. The case is about a man who sexually molested his daughter for many years. I gather it started when she was around eight. The accused has earlier pleaded guilty and now Judge Shillington gives him a two-year good behaviour bond. No jail time at all.

I'm home, I say to myself. This is going to be fine. We have a lenient judge. The lift breaking down was a blessing. It happened for a reason.

The mood is reasonably positive as my sentencing hearing gets under way. Because I am pleading guilty, the prosecution case is pretty simple. The Crown prosecutor, Chris O'Donnell, only calls one witness, a Federal Police officer who takes the stand to testify to the police statement of facts. Unfortunately, he is not the officer I usually deal with – she is on leave – so he is not entirely up on the details. But he is on the stand fairly briefly, and then it is over to the defence to show the judge why I should not go to jail.

I am the first defence witness to take the stand. I feel so little and nervous compared with my barrister, Elizabeth, a woman of strength and commanding intelligence, in her black robe and red slash of lipstick. I admire her power. Elizabeth takes me through the story, starting with Eddie's and my decision to go to India. She runs through my financial situation, the gold bullion, our holiday in Goa and how, even though I wasn't aware of it at the time, my early pregnancy in India was making me sick and emotional.

As we approach Eddie's announcement that he was bringing back the hash, my barrister goes into more and more detail. When her questions turn to the flight home and that terrible moment in the toilet I become aware of my body starting to tremble.

What was going through your mind at that time?

I was feeling a little bit upset about it.

A little bit upset?

I was a bit teary. (I am starting to cry now, too.)

Just contain yourself, please, and tell His Honour why you were feeling teary and why you were feeling upset?

Because I wanted to prove to him that I loved him so that's why I did that, I wanted him to love me ... He said ... If you really love me, this is one thing that you would do for me.

It is all I can do to keep my head up. I am humiliated and exhausted. Now everyone knows how weak I really am. I am someone who would break the law – risk everything I have – for a man.

The questions continue for the rest of the morning, and again after lunch. When my barrister is finished with me, the Crown prosecutor steps up to begin his cross-examination. Mostly he is interested in my financial affairs and trawling back through the minutiae of my bringing in the hash and lying to the police to cover for Eddie. It is awful and embarrassing, but I make it through to the end and feel I have held up pretty well. I don't act tough or soft. I am just empty. My belly feels like a watermelon.

Our second witness is the psychiatrist Dr William Barclay. He runs through my childhood and how it has affected me; my lack of bonding with others as a child and my subsequent need to be loved, my vulnerability and bad judgement when it comes to men. Taking all of that into account, my barrister asks him how it will affect me if I am sent to jail.

Dr Barclay answers: I believe it will be devastating, psychologically, for her. She sees the seventeen years she spent in orphanages as being an imprisonment. In many senses it was. She did abscond a number of times – [girls who did that] were taken back and treated quite harshly ... She regressed substantially in the short period of time she was in prison and became extremely depressed.

The barrister turns to the topic of the Valium that Eddie gave me on the plane. She asks: Have you ever prescribed Valium for a patient under your care?

Yes.

A 20 milligram dose of Valium: what effect psychologically would that have on a person who doesn't normally take it?

That knocks you out. I mean, that's the normal therapeutic dose of Valium. Normal daily dose is 5 milligrams, four times a day. It would bomb you out.

After sleeping, let us say for some hours and emerging out of sleep, would judgement, rationality or reason be in any way impaired?

You would certainly wake up pretty hung-over and still fairly sleepy. I wouldn't go so far as to say you would be irrational, but you would be knocked out by it.

From my seat behind the lawyers, everything seems to be going well. Even though, yes, I am guilty, surely the judge can see the circumstances that led me to make such a terrible mistake.

Last to take the stand is David Hanlon. He is a character witness, giving evidence about how honest and trustworthy he thinks I am, how close I am to my children and how Jessie, in particular, would suffer if I went to jail. He says how well regarded I am in the community and how shocked he was when he heard what I had done. He is so confident and unruffled on the stand; he does a brilliant job. It is the icing on the cake.

As David steps down, the lawyer hands the judge a pile of written character testimonials backing up David's evidence, along with a doctor's report on my pregnancy and obstetric history. Then suddenly it is all over. It has taken most of the day and we have done all we can. It is now in Judge Shillington's hands. He adjourns and says he will have a decision on 29 June. I have at least one more month of freedom.

25th May
I'm so relieved, last night I slept like a baby.
My God it's finally coming to an end. I feel
very positive about what will be the outcome.
Thank you Eliz Fullerton [barrister] you did a
wonderful job. I so much admire your strength.
What I would give to be like you, a strong com-
petent woman, you were not intimidated for one
minute by anyone in the court room.

Bill Barclay [psychiatrist]

If what you said was true I certainly need to
take a look at myself & my life. I must keep
away from men until I get to know who I really
am . . .

Today I feel totally exhausted. Everything
has reached a climax & I'm so tired. I really
need to prepare myself for the birth of my child
& get Jessie back home with me. My body is
aching, all the stress is coming out in pain all
down my back & chest.

9th June
I'm trying to be optimistic about 29th June . . .
Last night (full moon) I became very emotional. The next day I woke & there was blood,
then later in the day more blood. The doc says
they can save the baby if I go to Brisbane. I'm
on my own & I'm scared. No one is living with
me. I know I have friends but they are never
here when I need them, & where is Ed, travelling around Poona having a good time as he puts
it.

13th June
I'm not bleeding anymore, although I'm having painless contractions. Being up here on my own scares me somewhat, especially at night. I really need someone with me all the time now . . . I think I'm going crazy.

21 June
Eight days to go. Today I feel good for some reason, maybe because Dylan is coming down at long last. I just want to give Dylan all my time before I go to Sydney & to get through the week I have to believe I'm coming home after the 29th. How strange to think after all this time my life depends upon one single person, the judge. No one really knows what I've been through. How could they know.

I found out recently I'm having a boy. I've known all along but now it has been confirmed. Hello my sweet little one. I knew you when you were nameless. Before you were known to the world. I saw the days of your living before one of them was formed. I beheld you & loved you before you even knew the need of my love. I counted you worthy, I called you beautiful for I created you . . . I make this promise to you my darling now & forever, whenever you need me I will always be there. I grow to love you every day. At first I was a little scared to love you because of what lies ahead. Dear God, if there is one, let me have my baby boy in peace.

23rd

Dylan & I are going out to have a good time tonite. So we go to [my friend] Gwyn's on the way out. For some reason the lawyers had her number. I take the call. I'm told the judge has made a decision & I have to be in Syd Tues not Frid. That moment upon putting the phone down I suddenly got the shits really bad. My tummy went into spasms. I couldn't go out so we went & had hot choc & Ringoes . . . So now 4 days to go.

3 days to go, still I have the shits & my tummy is in spasm. The fear is unbelievable. I feel for this poor little boy inside my womb. I ask the barrister, is she confident still? Her answer: she hasn't given it another thought & won't until D-day. So detached, that lady, does she have to be so cold? It's so good having you here Dylan.

25th 5pm

Message on answering machine for me to go to Syd now as the Judge wants me in court tomorrow & come prepared to go to jail. Tears just start streaming down my face. Dylan is in bedroom. All I know is I must tell him what's going on. He says, Mum I'll ring you on Wed, so I say OK darling I'll speak to you then . . .

Since Frid I have been losing [fluid] & getting contractions. The doctor says it's fear & hopes I don't go into labour in Sydney. My God how much longer can I hang onto this precious thing. Stay with me baby I'll make it up to you.

I'm sorry for putting you through all this stress.

4am 26th June D-day
Wake with the worst pain in my heart after a bad nightmare. In my nightmare I went to jail 18 mths. My barrister could only say, Well you shouldn't have done it Donna. I can't get back to sleep, I lie here thinking. My brain is in overtime. People around me say you won't go to jail Donna, but if only they knew what agony I'm in. I just don't know if I'll get through this day... Poor Dylan, the look on your face, that's all I see when I think of you...

Jessie & Dylan I love you & I'm sorry.

CHAPTER 23

I am sitting in the dock of the District Court in Sydney, my seven-months pregnant belly resting on my thighs. I try to be positive. My lawyers are still pretty sure I will not go to jail: it is a first offence, I have pleaded guilty, I have shown remorse and told the police what they want to know. The expectation is that I will receive a fine or a suspended sentence.

Judge Shillington enters, wearing his wig and scarlet gown. He has a stern look on his face. We all stand. I look at this man – old and fat – who will decide my fate, and wonder what he thinks of me. Once everyone is again seated and the shuffling dies down, he looks down at his notes and begins to read. He speaks with authority, his voice hard and cold: Donna Lois Ehrenburg, you appeared before this Court on 24 May last when you pleaded guilty to a charge that you did import into Australia prohibited imports . . . I am satisfied on the evidence that, on your apprehension at Sydney airport, you were found to have . . . some 2.313 kilograms of cannabis resin. There is evidence before me that the street value of this material is in the order of $25,000. Clearly, the substantial amount involved would lead the court to the conclusion that the purpose of the importation was a commercial one.

SINS OF THE MOTHERS

I can barely concentrate on what he is saying, I feel so sick and tight with tension. I can feel my belly go rock hard. Hold on there, my little one.

Judge Shillington continues: It is clear that a man, Myatt, who is apparently overseas, was certainly very much involved ... [but] I was left with the distinct impression that there was an air of unreality about the account that you gave to this Court. I find it difficult to accept that Myatt would have delayed putting the proposition to assist him to you until you were almost back in Sydney ... I am satisfied, on the contrary, that this material was placed on [you] in India and that you were certainly involved in its purchase in India.

Oh God, it's not true. It's not true. I am telling you the truth. The judge is looking at me with such contempt, like I am a drug dealer. The lowest of the low. It is that orphanage feeling again; disgusting and smelly, alone and full of sin. I watch Judge Shillington looking at me and I wonder, does he not feel any compassion? Does he not see me as a human being? But he does not believe me. It's as simple as that.

Judge Shillington is still talking: I take into account a number of matters in your favour and in particular I take into account your plea of guilty before this court; the contrition which is evident by that plea. I also take into account the fact that you have indicated on oath that you are prepared to assist the authorities in any proceedings against the co-offender, Myatt. I take into account also that you have no previous convictions. You are now thirty-nine years of age. There is a further tragic complication, that you are presently pregnant and a child is due at the end of August of this year. I am also satisfied that, on the material placed before me, you are, in all other respects, a person of good character ... I bear in mind your upbringing. It is clear from the material put before me that you had a deprived childhood, your upbringing was one in which brutality was common. You [did

193

not have] a secure family life, but on the contrary, you were brought up in orphanages where love was completely lacking. You have had a failed marriage, you have had failed associations with other men, which have all obviously affected you, which is referred to by Dr Barclay. Dr Barclay's view is that incarceration for you would be a devastating experience.

Okay, I start telling myself, maybe it is going okay after all. This all sounds good. The lawyers are right when they say I am not going to jail. I will get a bond, a fine.

Judge Shillington: . . . but I am reluctantly drawn to the conclusion that the amount of cannabis involved, the nature of the offence and the need for general deterrence leads me to the conclusion that I must impose a custodial sentence.

My stomach lurches.

He asks me if I am well enough to stand.

Sure.

I can feel pain in my belly. Something is wrong. God, don't let me collapse in front of this judge.

Judge Shillington: On the charge upon which you have pleaded guilty, I sentence you to imprisonment for a minimum term of eighteen months, an additional term of six months. The terms are to date from today.

I want to fall over, drop to the floor. Two years. It takes all my strength to keep standing.

Suddenly there is a tangle of activity around me. Everyone is gathering, talking. *Oh my God, how did this happen?* The lawyers, my friends. It seems everyone is in shock, not just me. Even the prosecutor has her mouth open, as if to say: *She got a custodial sentence?* Because they didn't ask for a jail sentence. My friend Pam comes and puts her arms around me, and I just don't know what to say to people because I am so humiliated. All I can think is, What about the letter from the chamber magistrate? Doesn't that mean anything to the stupid judge?

I am still standing there when I become aware of warm fluid coming out of me and running down my leg. I am bleeding. Then a god-awful contraction grips my body. I just stand there frozen. I am welded to the floor. I can't take that step to walk out of the courtroom and I am embarrassed because I am bleeding.

Finally, I turn to Pam: There's something wrong. I'm having the baby. I'm definitely having the baby now. The prosecutor or someone turns around to Judge Shillington and says, She's unwell, Your Honour, and the judge says, Clear the courtroom, please. That is all I can hear. Clear the courtroom, please. He does not want to know.

So now I have to take a step to move but I can't walk. They are sort of helping me out. Two men cuff me and walk me down to a cell somewhere in the bowels of the courthouse. Clang the heavy metal doors shut and they walk away. I am alone.

I keep hearing the judge's words: Clear the courtroom, please. I wonder, who does the man go home to at night? Was he not with his wife when she had a baby? Has he not been with women who have been vulnerable? Has he not seen what a woman experiences when she goes into labour? Or did I give up my son's rights by doing what I did? Maybe I did. The judge must be a robot. He can't be a human being. I am losing the plot. Or have I lost it already?

My barrister turns up in her black robe, with her blood-red lips. We're going to start bail proceedings for you straightaway, she says. We're going to appeal.

Right this minute? I ask. Because I need help now.

I'm doing what I can, she snaps, and stalks out.

When a policeman turns up, I know I have to get through to him. Bloody hell, I'm in labour, I say. Do you want to have a look at the blood? I am actually in labour, I'm losing the baby.

He pauses.

We'd better call an ambulance.

CHAPTER 24

After court
18 months jail the judge hander done I can't write or spell fuck I'm freaked out. I'm bleeding I'm scared, what to do I don't know someone help me . . . anyone. I now have no rights. They gave me no lunch I'm in pain. Judge Shillington how could you do this. The ambulance has arrived they are taking me to hospital. I don't feel too good, the contractions are coming every 5 min, the doctor says I'm in labour, they must stop it if they can, so now they drip me up with Ventolin. I can't write I'm shaking I can't spell, I can't remember things how I left the court how I got here, I think I'm in shock, I'm scared really scared please someone take me home I want my Dylan & Jessie, the baby is coming too soon.

It is 26 June. My mother's birthday. Now my baby wants to be born on this day.

I am still having irregular contractions and a little bit of bleeding late in the afternoon. A doctor asks me if I want to have the baby. Isn't it too early? I am only thirty-one and a half weeks – eight and a half weeks to go. Please hold on, little one. I am so frightened.

I think back to an ultrasound I had just ten days ago. The baby looked perfect. I could see his beautiful long fingers and his little nose. I keep telling myself, Physically he is okay. At least, physically he is going to be okay.

They have brought me to St Margaret's Hospital, in inner-city Surry Hills, hooked up to a Ventolin drip. Ventolin relaxes the uterus, which stops the contractions and so suppresses labour. The paediatrician here doesn't want the baby born yet, either. It is hospital policy. The nursery is not equipped to deal with a premmie under thirty-two weeks. Under normal circumstances they would transfer me to a hospital with a more high-tech nursery, but apparently there are no beds available nearby. Maybe it is because I come with an entourage of police guards. St Margaret's tries to arrange a transfer to Westmead instead, twenty-odd kilometres away near Parramatta in the western suburbs, but for whatever reason they won't accept me there either. There is no choice for me but to remain at St Margaret's, with two police officers stationed outside my door. I wonder what the other women in labour must think.

27th
Up all nite. The Ventolin gives you heart pal-
pitations & the shakes. Pam comes to see me, all
of a sudden 2 cops barge in. I was checking my
pad for fluid as Pam was told my waters had broken, so the cops wanted to look in my bed. I
told them to go away but no they want to stay
in room & stare. I have to keep writing as when

197

```
I go to jail they will take my book away. Appeal
please Liz Fullerton. They say they can reduce
sentence to ½ at least. Please God let that be.
How ironic, the dream the nite before came true
. . .
    I'm shaking because I'm still in shock. My
writing is weird, the brain not working.
```

The nurse writes on my chart that I am distressed and gives me some Normison to help me sleep. The drugs finally send me off. Some relief from this nightmare . . .

In the morning I am losing more fluid, only this time it is green. The nurse wonders whether it is meconium, the baby's first poo. I have had enough babies to know that this could be a sign the baby is in distress and needs to be born. If any other woman in here was leaking green fluid, the nurses would be alert to the situation in an instant; that is one of the main things they are constantly checking for. But now it is happening to Mary Fishpot, nobody does anything about it. Another nurse later describes the loss as greenish brown sludgish – and yet still virtually nothing is done. A brief once-over and then I am left to lie here alone, my head whirring with fear. I feel like everything has been taken out of my hands. I have no control. I am only a prisoner, a criminal.

I am allowed a phone call from the kids. Dylan is bubbling with questions. I can hear the tremble in his voice: What's happening, Mum? How's the bail application going, Mum? When are you coming home? He is fifteen and all of a sudden he has to grow up.

Jessie is only eleven. She gets on the phone.

Mummy?

And I am trying to pretend that I am all right but I can't talk. I try but I just can't.

Later that night, labour starts up again. More strong contractions. Test results show that I have a Gardnerella infection, which I gather is a possible reason for early labour. Then again, maybe it is all the stress. Can stress send you into early labour? They pump more Ventolin into me to try to stave off the labour but that feels even worse. I am not optimistic about the baby. They say thirty-two weeks is very early. I am sorry, little one, it has all been too much for me.

Even with me in an unstable condition, the prison authorities try to have me transferred to the medical facility within the jail. Fortunately, it does not accept patients on drips or in threatened premature labour, so I will remain at St Margaret's, at least for now. As a compromise, Corrective Services are going to send their own guards to replace the police officers stationed outside my door.

28th June
I'm now under Corrective Services dept & they seem, well I'm not sure yet. Last night was a worry, I really thought the babe was coming. I'm getting scared, I'm only allowed one visit a week & one phone call . . .

I can't keep writing in this book much longer because I have to hand it over because I may have something hidden in the cover.

I have pushed my fate beyond the limits this time. I have got myself into so much trouble. I can't keep blaming Eddie, I played a part too. If I'm to stay alive I must accept my fate.

I can't sleep. I close my eyes and everything comes to me. Jail, loss of Dylan & Jessie. I'm getting contractions. No one is here. I'm in a room with two corrective services people who

have the light on all nite. I've lost everything
. . . Tears tears tears & more. Pain pain & more
pain. Will it ever stop? I just want to go on
a long sleep & wake to find it all over.
Otherwise I don't want to wake.

One of the guards has gone outside for a smoke, so I am left
alone in my room with a male guard. Just him and me. Then a
nurse comes in to tell the male guard that he has a phone call.
Under no circumstances am I to be left alone, but he wants to
take the call, so he gets out his handcuffs and chains me to the
bed. Please do not cuff me to the bed, I say. I'm not going to go
anywhere, I've got a drip in my arm.

It's procedure, he says.

So I have one arm with a drip in it and another cuffed to the
bed. The nurse looks at me crying. She even says to the guard,
That won't be necessary, Donna is too sick to go anywhere.

But he walks out.

The Corrective Services guards keep reminding me that I am
in prison. I might physically be in the hospital but I am actually
in jail. They control my life now. They are with me always, two
new guards every six hours. Two chairs at the end of my bed.
They sit in my room rather than outside in the corridor, because
in here they can smoke in the toilet and watch the telly.

The nurses come in to check my pad, and the guards – often
men – just sit there. I feel completely humiliated. I plead with
them for my privacy but I am just a prisoner. An orphan. What
can I do? All the guards can say is that this is nothing compared
to how hard jail will be.

There is a lot of discussion between the medical staff and
Corrective Services about my care. I am never included in any of
it. Corrective Services are pushing for me to be transferred to
Westmead, because it is near the jail. The guards keep telling me

how expensive it is for them to come all the way to St Margaret's. The overtime and travel expenses are adding up.

Finally, Westmead agrees to accept me. So, the nurses ramp up the Ventolin and move me out of the labour ward ready for transfer the following morning. Suppress the labour, stabilise her, and get her out – those are basically the orders. It seems to me that Corrective Services are making my medical decisions.

The Ventolin makes me feel sick, though. My chest and back ache so that I cannot think clearly. I can't move. Consequently, they take me off the drip and an hour later the contractions come again, ten minutes apart.

I am in and out of labour throughout the night, the guards all I have in the way of support. Some of the nurses seem too afraid to come into my room. I get the feeling they are intimidated by the guards. Not that I can blame them.

The guards volunteer to time my contractions – the female guard is seven months pregnant and wants to practise – and, apparently, the nurses give them permission. The contractions are getting stronger and more painful, so I ask the guards to call a nurse.

No, the nurses are busy.

Then I start to bleed and ask again for the nurse.

Don't worry, says the guard. You'll be okay.

By morning the bleeding is getting heavy by the time someone finally comes in to check on me. When the nurse sees I am losing clots, she realises how serious my condition is.

The doctor is called and confirms there is active bleeding, which is not good. She says I am now unsuitable for transfer to Westmead. Instead, I am once again returned to the labour ward. I feel like a tatty old rag doll, being pushed and pulled every which way, with no one ever considering for one moment what is best for my baby. I even ask the guards if I can bring in a private doctor. I will pay for it. But they tell me no, I am now under their care and they are making the decisions for me, so I had better get used to it.

Since they are keeping me here, the doctor re-examines me and decides to perform an emergency Caesarean. I am instructed not to eat any breakfast in anticipation of surgery.

As I am prepped and changed into a fresh gown, my nerves start to get the better of me. The baby is too little to be born. Please, God, let him be okay. Just let him be placed safe and well in my arms so I can protect him.

I am waiting outside the operating theatre, the two guards in tow, when a nurse approaches me with a confused look on her face. She says that, actually, I will no longer be having the Caesarean.

I am wheeled back to the labour ward feeling utterly confused. The Ventolin drip goes back up. The bleeding has stopped. The baby will not be born today after all.

Hang in there, darling. I love you. Maybe the bail will come through and you can be born in peace.

29th June
I feel at any moment I'm going to crack . . .

I don't want to clean my teeth wash my hair clean my body what for I hate myself for what has happened. I gave all my power away to Eddie. Fuck I must be crazy . . . I am crazy.

Jessie I was writing this book for you, as I know you wouldn't care about my spelling or composition & not to mention the writing, but things have changed & now it's just a book about a tragic year of my life.

30th June
I've just heard if Jessie or Dylan come to see me they will have to be searched, open their mouth & go through a metal detector. I really don't think I should see them. I feel too ashamed to have them see me this way . . .

Without my Dylan & Jessie there is an emptiness in my life . . .

In the room next to me there is a delivery going on. The woman is screaming blue murder but my God she pushed the baby out. I can't stand to look at these guards anymore. I wish they would go away.

1st July
Just woke. All I'm certain of now is when I open my eyes there will be 2 guards sitting on chairs watching me around the clock . . .

Sometimes I fantasise that I'm a celebrity & they are protecting me but moments later the reality hits me.

2nd July
Couldn't sleep last night with all the chatter going on, lights, guards & baby after baby being born, the ladies screaming . . .

I ask to go to toilet. I'm 53kg, 7 months pregnant, very weak, can hardly walk. Yet 2 guards follow me, one in front one behind. How pathetic I must look. I'm told any minute now I'm going to Westmead. It's Mon & I can't have any more phone calls this week.

After six nights in St Margaret's, they dope me up on Ventolin and load me onto an ambulance for the drive out to Westmead Hospital. I am escorted by a doctor, a nurse and, of course, a guard, who handcuffs me inside the ambulance. It is procedure.

We arrive at Westmead at around 11.30 am and the first thing the doctor asks me is, Why has St Margaret's suppressed your labour for so long?

Because I was only thirty-one weeks pregnant, I tell him.

That's not a reason, he says. We deliver babies from twenty-six weeks.

So now there is a big discussion between all the doctors about what to do with me. Caesarean? Stop the Ventolin? If I have a Caesarean the recovery time is longer so I get to spend more time with my baby. This is what it has come down to: a matter of days with my baby. I am too sick to get involved.

They finally turn to me: Donna, we are taking you off the Ventolin. You're having this baby today. I am wheeled straight to the labour ward, my two guards trailing.

The waves of contractions build. I look out the window and imagine I see Dylan and Jessie playing. All I want to do is touch them, call to them. I wish I could take away their pain. Now I have to decide who to give my baby to. If only someone was with me.

```
How crazy am I here in labour writing away . . .
If it's one consolation I will at least have a
beautiful boy. I just want to hold him, put him
on my breast, my baby.
```

The nurse gives me a sedative. She draws the curtains, dims the lights and tells me to try to relax into my labour. Then she shows me the buzzer, tells me to press it if I need something, and leaves.

The guards are decent enough to stand just outside the door. Having your baby under guard is a horrible thing for a mother. I lie here quietly crying. This is it, I am going to have the baby.

Suddenly the doors swing open and two new female guards barge into the room.

What is going on in here? one of them demands. This prisoner is supposed to have a guard watching her at all times.

The guards due to clock off are still right outside my door. They try to tell the new guards that I am not going anywhere, I am about to have a baby, but the aggressive guard is having none of it.

You seem to think, Ehrenburg, that you are in hospital, but you are, in actual fact, in jail. You are under our care and I don't care what's going on here, the lights stay on and those blinds are open.

So the fluoros come back on, with the glare of the afternoon sun, and the two new guards take their seats at the end of my bed for the birth of my baby.

My whole body tenses up. I beg them to sit outside the door, to please give me my privacy while I labour. But they will not leave the room. The aggressive one is actually excited because she has never seen a baby being born before.

And that is when I lose it. I start shaking, screaming at them. Get out! Get out! For God's sake, I am in labour. Just get out and leave me alone! LEAVE ME ALONE! I am completely out of control, I simply can't deal with it anymore. I am at breaking point.

In the end I am sobbing and the nurse comes in to see what is going on. She calls the doctor and he gives me another sedative. As I start to zone out, I can hear the medical staff negotiating with the guards.

She is not going to run away, she's in labour. You can wait right outside her door.

We've got our orders and we are not to let her out of our sight for a minute.

This is not a jail, this is a labour ward. Donna needs to give birth in peace.

We are staying right here in this room.

They are going on and on and I am crying and thinking, Fuckin' hell, this is worse than an orphanage. How did I get here? What have I done? For love? For Eddie? I know I did wrong but the price is too high.

The guards eventually agree to sit in the open doorway. They can still see me, but at least it is better than having them at the end of my bed.

As night falls, my contractions come on harder and faster. The guards chatter away. It is so bad. Not the pain. The pain I can handle. It is knowing that I am in here with these guards. That my child will be born in custody. My last child. My baby. And all the while they are telling me, You are not going to breastfeed the baby. You will have the baby for one hour, then the baby will be taken from you and you will be transferred to the prison hospital.

Oh.

Sometime in the evening, a nurse comes to me and says, Let us ring someone, you really need to have someone here for you. You'll be able to do that, I promise you. Who do you know that we can call to come and be with you?

I don't know, I'm from Byron Bay. There's nobody, really.

But it turns out a woman I know from Byron, Liz Mason, is in Sydney, and she manages to make it out to Westmead by about 9.30 pm. Dylan and her son are good friends. At least I have someone by my side now.

It is the darkest hour of the morning – suicide hour – and I am still in labour. Delirious. The midwife is saying to me, You are about to give birth to your baby, Donna. You are going to have

206

to push. And I am asking, Am I going to have the baby today? Am I having a baby?

You are having the baby any minute now, Donna. I need you to push.

It takes just one push and this tiny baby flops out. Liz is standing by my side and starts to cry. She is sobbing. I think she must be overcome by the joy of the birth so I say to her, Is this a really good experience for you, watching me give birth? Is that why you're crying?

She pauses.

Yeah.

And then I know.

Something is wrong with the baby, isn't it?

CHAPTER 25

All I can see is his little hand sticking up. I look at the hand and it is scabby. Rotting.

The doctor is examining the hand and says, It's all right, Mrs Ehrenburg, he's just missing a few fingers and toes.

Just like that. *Oh, it's all right, he's just missing a few fingers and toes.*

Liz is holding my hand. She is still crying. But I am thinking, No, he's not missing a few fingers and toes. I saw him on the ultrasound. He is okay. Physically, he is okay. I remember so clearly. So clearly.

But yes, I can see this rotting hand, all scabby. I can still see it when I close my eyes now.

Is he okay? Is he okay? Over and over in my head.

No, he's not okay. We don't know. We have to take the baby away now.

They wrap him in foil and whisk him off to the newborn intensive care unit.

He is gone without any further explanation.

Baby born 3.30am 3 July Tues
4lb baby deformed hands & feet. I just want to
die. Please take me now . . .

I haven't touched him or seen him. They just
took him away. Still don't know if there is anything else wrong. I'm alone in labour ward 5am.
I feel ashamed, baby malnourished. It was all
too much for him. Thank you Liz, you were great.
My depression, I don't know how far it goes, how
deep. I just can't believe it, they have just
left me sitting in a wheelchair.

5.30 I still haven't touched the babe. I'm
confused as to how I feel emotionally . . . I
have to be very honest when I say I don't want
him. I've rejected him, I'm scared of him, it's
not my child. They fed the guards before they
fed me. The Corrective Service only will allow
2 phone calls today & then no more till 7 days.
They are keen for me to suffer.

A nurse comes in and says, Get up and have a shower.

I can't, I say.

Go and have a shower, one of the guards butts in.

I remember thinking when I had Dylan and Jessie how well
the midwives take care of you. But no one is taking care of me
this time.

I try to get up to have a shower, but suddenly everything goes
blank and I wake up on the floor. It's all right Mrs Ehrenburg,
you just fainted. The nurse gets me back into bed. I am not well,
I tell her, I am just not well. I am crying and she must have some
compassion because she says, I'll take care of you. She cleans me
up. Gently wipes my body with a warm cloth while tears roll
down my face.

They wheel me up to the ward, to a private room where I can be on my own. With a new shift of guards, of course. One of the guards has long, dark hair and she tells me that the prison only wants me to spend one hour with the baby. I ask her why and she says it is to prevent me bonding with him because they don't want to have to deal with me being an emotional wreck when I get to prison.

But what about my poor baby? He needs me.

You should have thought about that before you broke the law. You did this to your baby. It's substance abuse. It's your own fault.

And deep down I agree with her because I did do this to my baby. It is not substance abuse, but I did do this to him with the stress of this whole nightmare. My own left hand is useless and now my baby's hand is deformed. Was it all those childhood prayers in the orphanage?

Please God deform me in any way but don't let me wet the bed.

It has come back to haunt me.

Please God deform me in any way but don't let me wet the bed.

I am so numb. I don't know what is happening. All I know is that the baby was born with fingers and toes missing. How did it happen? How could my son not have fingers and toes? They say he might have brain damage too, the doctors don't know yet. All they can tell me is that it is a wait-and-see situation.

3pm Still haven't touched the babe or connected . . . I'm sorry Jess & Dylan I've let you down again. I couldn't even have a healthy child. How can I bring babe home & be proud, show him off to everyone, my perfect babe. But something went terribly wrong. The doc says I should get closer to my child. I wake from sleep & just for a short moment I thought it was a dream . . .

The guards won't let me speak to anyone. I need
to talk about the babe. The people I need the
most I have been cut off from. No visits, no
phone calls. I want to hold this little one but
all those tubes & that hand all I see is his
[missing fingers] & I feel sick. I need someone.

7.30 I went to see babe. He had so many tubes
sticking out you couldn't see the face. I'm told
he's not only [missing fingers and toes] he's
very sick . . .

Above the sink in my room is a hand sign for
germs. The perfect hand. I keep seeing the hand
when I wake & then I think of the baby . . .

A new guard comes in and washes her hands. She looks up at the
hand-washing sign above the sink. Look at those perfect hands,
she says. Ehrenburg's baby doesn't have perfect hands.

And I just think, No, he doesn't have perfect hands.

I am wheeled in to see a paediatrician. The first thing she asks
me is, What is your crime?

I tell her I brought in hash from India for someone. It was a
crime of passion.

Then you are worse than the dealers, she says.

She cannot see past what I've done. In her eyes, I am scum.

They still cannot diagnose my baby. He has scars that look as
though there are tight elastic bands around his hand and foot –
constriction rings, they call it – and he is missing fingers and toes
with just big dried scabs in their place. More fingers look like
they will fall off, and toes are fused together. The paediatrician
suggests his injuries might be from something called amniotic
bands.

How did it happen? I ask.

We don't know yet. It is probably just bad luck.

Just bad luck.

Anyway, she adds, it is best you adopt the baby out.

I look at her, searching for something more, but she just says, That will be all.

4th July

Breast milk, it won't come, I wonder why. Had a shower, only out of respect for Eliz. Fullerton . . .

The baby still in Intensive Care. Maybe today he will start holding on his own. In my eyes the baby wants to die. Going to see babe, guards behind me. I see the babe, guards looking over my shoulder. I just want privacy, be alone with babe. Please just give me 5 min, but no. I walk past Chapel. I want to go in, be with God & ask why but I can't because I can't be alone with him. The doctor comes in, says hi to guards & reads my notes then walks out. You see now I'm just a common prisoner, not Donna.

My opinion of the babe, he was in my womb, found out whilst there his mum was suffering so bad he couldn't bear to stay with me . . . I should have let him come then let him die. I feel that's what he wanted. He did not want to come into this world, would you?

I feel I have done this to you. I'm told I didn't. They get 2 cases a year. It's just bad luck, Bad Luck . . .

Michael just called, yet another lawyer. Said my chances were good on bail. Tony Bellanto [QC] you better do the job. Help me I'm begging you.

A friend from Byron Bay, Leo Doublecross, bowls in to my room with an enormous bunch of yellow roses. My favourite flower. It reminds me of when Jessie was born and Robert filled my room with them.

Leo is all smiles and warmth, and, What can I do for you, Donna?

He has quite a presence, Leo. He doesn't give a damn about the guards and they immediately back off. They see him in his expensive suit, a rich, private-school boy with all his top-end-of-town contacts, and they don't even search him.

So what do you want me to do? he asks.

Get me out of here.

There is no emotional stuff with Leo, he just says, Consider it done!

He is so confident, for a minute I feel as though I have a little bit of strength.

Truly, Donna, what else can I do? he asks.

I don't know what to do anymore, I say. I'm stuck here.

Where's the baby?

I want to tell him something is wrong, to explain, but I can't find the words. Instead I just say, I haven't even touched the baby.

I want to see the baby, he says.

I don't think that's allowed, I say.

But he has already called a nurse: I want a wheelchair. And before I can resist, he is bundling me up in his arms. Come on, up. Out of that bed. You're coming with me.

He turns to the guards: I take it she's allowed to see her baby?

Yeah, I suppose. But we don't advise it.

Leo won't be deterred. Well, then, if you want to join the entourage, let's go. And he wheels me off down the corridor like he has all the power in the world.

The four of us stand at the window of the Special Care

nursery, looking in at the sick little babies in their humidicribs. A nurse approaches and tells me it would be good if I touched my baby, so Leo and I wash our hands and put on gowns to go inside. The guards follow us into the sterile environment without bothering to do either. Then they stand over my shoulder muttering, Look at those fingers.

My little baby looks better today. Now he only has a tube in his nose, a heart monitor and a drip in his hand and foot. He doesn't make a sound. I feel a tingle of hope but then I notice that across the front of his humidicrib is a sign: SUBSTANCE ABUSE BABY.

I break down: Leo, tell them I'm not a substance abuse mother, it's not true. Tell them.

We'll take care of that, he says. But how about we touch the baby first.

I am too scared to touch the baby. Too scared I might love him and then have to let him go. But Leo turns to a nurse: Can we take the baby for a minute? Surely we can take the baby out of the humidicrib.

So he does. He takes him and his tangle of tubes out of the crib, and nurses my tiny bundle. I wonder, does he see what is wrong? He is the first person to show my baby some love. Then he turns to me and places him on my lap.

It is the first time I have held my child. I am so overcome with all the awe, love and fear I feel that I am almost paralysed. And then, in less than a minute, the nurse returns. Already?

That's enough now, she says. We have to put the baby back.

She takes the baby from me and I begin to cry. It is too much to cope with.

The nurse must see how hard this is because she turns back towards me and gently takes my hand. She guides it through a hole in the humidicrib, placing it onto the baby. You can still touch him, she says.

214

His little chest heaves and jerks. His eyes are closed. He looks so fragile. And the tiny hand . . . the little finger is all that is left and even it is black and dying.

But reaching into the crib to touch his healthy hand I am shocked at the strength with which he grasps my finger. He holds on to me so tightly that it jolts me out of my hopelessness. His strength is my strength.

And so, there in the Special Care nursery, holding hands and with the bleeping sounds of life support surrounding us, I make a pact with my baby.

It's you and me together, little one. Mummy's here.

The first part of the deal is to get us both out of custody.

```
Yellow  roses . . . Leo  Doublecross  you  beauty.
You  made  my  day  seeing  your  face,  helping  me.
Talk  about  action.  You  brought  me  to  my  babe.
You  broke  down  the  guards  real  quick.  You  were
the  first  person  to  nurse  my  babe.  You  are  his
godfather,  you  gave  me  hope.
```

CHAPTER 26

There are so many things I must do and suddenly I am full of the need for action. I have to get my baby well, I have to get bail so I can take him home. At least I am excused from appearing in court at the moment, because I am too ill; my lawyers can do that without me.

I also have to clear up this awful lie that my son is a substance abuse baby. I have not even drunk tea since I discovered I was pregnant. I haven't drunk coffee, I don't smoke cigarettes, I don't drink wine, I don't do anything. I have been a complete and utter recluse. My name tag reads Mulawa Detention Centre and because of that I have been discriminated against. That is one thing, but they are not going to discriminate against my baby, too. I am so angry with the nurses for writing SUB-STANCE ABUSE BABY on my son's humidicrib. I beg them to take down the sign. I say to the nurse, Did you find any drugs in my urine?

She says, No.

So I ask, Why, then?

She just looks at me. What can she say?

I meet with a new paediatrician, Dr David Thomas. He is

calm and tender and we have a long talk. He doesn't judge me for one second. I say to him, I don't know why they've done this because my son is not a substance abuse baby.

Dr Thomas says, I know that, Donna. I know he's not a substance abuse baby.

So I say, Well, I need you to go to the nurses, and to my records, and I need you to write that down.

He immediately turns to a nurse and says, Get rid of that sign, please; he is not a substance abuse baby. All drug screening tests are negative.

It is my first small victory.

Dr Thomas sits at the end of my bed and asks the guards for some time alone with me. They retreat as far as the door.

He looks at me and before he has a chance to speak I say, It's genetic, isn't it? I feel so guilty that my damaged genes have done this to my child. Look at this, I say, offering my pathetic left hand for inspection. It's no good.

What happened? he asks.

I think it happened when I fell off a swing when I was about ten, I say. A doctor has since told me that someone must have strapped the bandage on too tight, which caused nerve damage.

Listen, Donna, Dr Thomas says, it's not genetic. We don't know yet what has happened to your baby, but whatever has happened, it has only just happened. Probably in the last three or four days.

How do you know that?

Because it's still happening, he says. Your baby is still losing fingers and toes. His hand may still come off. He may even lose a leg. We just don't know yet.

Dr Thomas explains to me about amniotic bands, the most likely diagnosis. He says that the baby's fingers and toes probably dropped off because fibres, or 'bands', from the amniotic sac had wrapped around his extremities, constricting his blood supply.

217

What happens is, something causes a tear in the amniotic membrane, and, like a ripped pair of jeans, the edges start to fray until fibres break away. Then in the watery environment of the womb those fibres wrap themselves around whatever they find. Which in my baby's case, were his right hand and foot.

There are no other obvious abnormalities at this stage, according to Dr Thomas, but we will have to wait twelve months to see whether he has any brain damage. In the meantime, the baby will need to stay in hospital for about three weeks – or until he can be fed without tubes – and he will need to have surgery on his hand and foot. There is an added complication in that, under normal circumstances they would transfer us to the Children's Hospital, but apparently because I am a prisoner they can't do that.

Why can't they see that my baby is innocent?

5th
7am. I actually made contact with my babe. I love you darling. No matter you have minor defects, so what. You & I have a special bond darling & so will Dylan & Jessie. I'm sorry I rejected you & couldn't touch you. I was so freaked out, just by the whole tragic situation. I know the judge is going to let me go home with you. I know he will give me my freedom. You need me now more than ever. I lie here trying to accept the situation.
Rosie just walked in . . .

My friend Rosie arrives with her two children, Narin and Melanie. What a buzz. I am so thrilled to see them. Rosie is one of my closest and oldest friends and we have known each other for twenty years. I met Rosie in Thailand in 1972 and stayed with her when I was pregnant with Dylan. She is strong and warm, and today I need her strength more than ever. I need to talk about the baby. Also, she is a nurse so I know she will help me understand what is going on. But straightaway, the guards ruin everything.

We've gotta search them, one says.

Melanie is just thirteen. The male guards touch her right down her body, down her breasts. Tears roll down her face. I say to the guards, You don't have to do this. Then I look at Rosie and say, Rosie, don't come. Please don't let your children come here. I don't want them to experience this.

But she says, No, it's important they see what it is all about, Donna.

Rosie and the kids keep my mind occupied while I await a phone call from my lawyers. They are in court without me today – my sixteenth court date – appealing for bail. I feel positive the judge will let me go home with my baby, but Rosie doesn't want me to get my hopes up.

It's 12.30, still no word from court. I wait with such anticipation. Sometime before 3 I'll know. It's so good to see Rosie. We nursed the babe, he is so fragile. He is 100% dependent upon me. I'm scared I've bonded with babe & I'm going to have to leave him.

It's 2 pm & I'm still waiting for word. I try to visualise what's going on in court. Creative visualisation.

I just stood under shower for $\frac{1}{2}$ hour trying to milk for babe. I can't seem to get any (stress) . . .

5pm. Lawyer just called. DPP will let bail go through, it's now up to Judge Studdert, Supreme

Court, tomorrow. I hear it's looking better.
One more night, I mustn't get my hopes up. I
think I am . . .

I long for a good night's sleep, where the
lights are out & the guards are gone . . .

What do I call this babe? Come on Donna give
him a name.

The nurses say the baby is still too weak to suck so they will not
let me breastfeed. He is only two and a half days old and being
fed by tubes, but I long to give him something myself. Just to
hold him, bring him into bed with me, tell him how much I love
him and be at peace. I need to protect him. I may have to leave
him soon and what will I have given him?

I know I can get him through this with my love and my milk.
I say to the paediatrician, Dr Thomas: I just want to put the baby
to my breast and no one will let me do it. I'm not going to hurt
him. Do you think they can trust me for one minute?

Sure, they can do that, he says.

So I go down to the nursery, and they get the baby out and put
him on my breast. I breastfed Jessie and Dylan for over a year
each so I know what I am doing. I can see him sucking, I am sure
he is drawing out the milk, but the nurse says to me, No, no, he's
too tired, he hasn't developed a sucking reflex yet. And they take
the baby back from me.

All I know is that this baby needs me more than even I can
understand. He is helpless.

Back in my room, Dr Thomas can see how desperate I am to
do something, so he says that we can still give the baby my milk,
I will just have to express and give it to him through the tube up
his nose and into his tummy.

The nurses bring me an electric pump, a video of a woman
breastfeeding and some Polaroids of my baby. Dr Thomas says

that looking at the video and the pictures of my baby will stimulate my milk.

So I watch the video with the suction cup attached to my breast and the rhythmic sound of the machine pumping away. The guards can't help themselves: She sounds like a cow, doesn't she, one sniggers.

How they can be this cruel is beyond me.

Even though I am expressing milk for the baby, when I am allowed to hold him and the nurses aren't watching, I still put him to my breast. I can see he is drinking the milk. When the nurses catch me, I tell them, Look, the milk is coming! It's flowing. But they reply, No, he's not getting any, he's only thirty-two weeks, he hasn't developed a sucking reflex.

But he is, I know.

But the standard procedure –

I don't give a shit about standard procedure. My baby is sucking.

Dr Thomas returns to see me and I ask him, If you could just let me have five minutes on each side. I know what I am doing, I need to do this. I'll be leaving him, and I need to give him something.

He says, Sure, whatever you want, you do it.

At last I am able to sit here nursing my baby. Yeah, I think, this is okay.

The guards still stand over my shoulder joking about substance abuse and missing fingers – they won't even stand outside the nursery and watch me through the glass – but I am not about to let them take this moment from me.

Occasionally, they wander off to look at the other babies. We are in Special Care with some very sick children and these guards are walking around with all their germs. They aren't wearing gowns, haven't washed their hands. At the same time I am thinking, Go, go to all the other babies. Just give me my peace.

It's funny, really, when you have a child. While you are

pregnant, there are all these moments of doubt: will I love this child as much as my other children? Can I cope with another baby? But then you give birth and somehow you fall completely in love all over again. And with this little one, especially, I feel a closeness, a protectiveness, that I didn't feel with the others. He is so fragile. He has no one but me.

He is just four days old and I am scared I am getting too close.

I am trying to pass the time, waiting for a decision about my bail.

The guards want to go outside for a smoke.

Get up, they order me.

I can't walk, I say.

We'll wheel you, then.

So they get me into a wheelchair and push me down the corridor to a windy verandah where they can smoke their cigarettes and chat away like I am not even there. It is the middle of July and I am freezing in my nightgown. But I do not want to upset these people because I know if I do I will be in worse trouble when I get to jail. At least I have my diary with me.

```
6th July 90
Supreme Court. Bail today?
    Court again 17th time. 5am 6th July. My first
thought was the baby . . .
    I'm at present sitting in the cold air so the
guards can have a smoke. I give them what they
want so I can have phone calls.

9.30am I'm trying so hard to keep it together.
I'm just waiting for court decision, trying to
stay calm. Milk is coming. I desperately need a
positive decision . . .
```

12 midday. Still no word. I'm sitting on a time bomb. The guards on this shift are OK. Rosie, where are you? Come & see me. I have to be positive, positive. My babe needs me.

LEO CALLED. You beauty, I'm going home. I got bail. Leo Doublecross [thank you]. I'm elated. I feel so good. My God I feel fantastic . . .

I'm free I'm free. $20,000 plus 150,000 from Leo & daily reporting . . .

<u>A new beginning. I'm free.</u>

CHAPTER 27

I am still waiting for Mulawa officials to bring papers for me to sign and to relieve the guards. They are driving me crazy. My lawyer explains that even though bail has been granted, the paperwork will not go through until Leo and I come up with the money. I have to put up $20,000 security, but Leo has to come up with $150,000. It could be a slow process and in the meantime I remain a prisoner, stuck with the guards. All I can do is dream of the moment they are gone. At least now I have that to look forward to. Just think, I will be able to sleep with the lights out, no chatter going on, walk where I want, have people bring food, hold my baby without being watched.

The conditions of my bail are that I must report daily by phone to police. I am also to surrender my passport and not go within 5 kilometres of the boundary of any airport or recognised point of departure for overseas. I am not going anywhere. I would never betray Leo's trust.

The Supreme Court judge apparently said that this whole situation is so tragic, how could he refuse bail?

The wonderful paediatrician, Dr Thomas, stops by to tell me how well my baby is doing. He is now strong enough that it will only be a few days before the two of us can be airlifted to Lismore Base Hospital, closer to home.

Two days after the judge has granted me bail, news finally comes through that the money has been raised and the paperwork is done. Suddenly the guards are transformed. It is all, Oh, Donna, isn't that wonderful. That's brilliant news ... but you know, it's a Friday afternoon, and we were really relying on getting paid overtime. It's the weekend ... You'd still be free and you can't leave the hospital anyway, so maybe we could work something out. We could put off the paperwork until Monday.

I am not sure I understand what I am hearing. I ask them, So are you saying that, right now, if I wanted to, I could get up out of this bed, walk out of here, and you wouldn't have to follow me?

And they say, Yeah, but we were just hoping we could come to some sort of arrangement so we could stay and get a bit more overtime.

I can't get out of the bed anyhow, but that is it. WELL, GET THE HELL OUT OF MY ROOM! GET OUT! GET OUT! GET OUT! NOT ONE MORE SECOND DO I WANT YOU IN MY ROOM. NOT ONE MORE SECOND.

GET ... OUT!

10.7.90
I woke this morning, I noticed the rays of sunlight shining through my room. I felt free.
Guards gone, clean on the inside somehow, peace
flooded over me, I was alive. (Babe now 1840
grams).

At last my baby and I can be together in peace. He needs so much from me. Dr Thomas says he has a long journey ahead of him and if I can continue to breastfeed him it will really help. So I start spending all my time in the nursery, sitting in a chair by his humidicrib. I am too weak to lift him out myself, so when it is time to feed him I press a buzzer to call the nurse and she hands him to me. Then when I am done, I press the buzzer again. I long for the day when he leaves the little cavern of his humidicrib for good so I can hold him day in and day out, try to make up for all the pain he has been through.

In the meantime, I want to do all that I can to help him. I have to get active. So, when my baby is not in my arms, I start massaging him. I reach into his humidicrib and run a finger down his spine, stroke him. And I can see his body responding to my touch. I know it must be stimulating something good in him. And, really, it is amazing how quickly he starts to grow strong.

A doctor comes to see me. He looks at me and says, You are well enough to be discharged.

It is quite obvious that I am not – I have a raised temperature and terrible back pains – but I see the way he looks at me. I try to tell him I can't even get out of bed. I am definitely not well. Whether it is physical, emotional, I don't know, but my body has had enough. I need to stay in the hospital.

He doesn't care.

And what about the baby? I ask.

He has to stay here, he says.

So how will I feed him?

You will have to come to the hospital each day.

But I've got nowhere to stay in Sydney.

Then you'll have to go back to Byron Bay.

Then how the hell am I going to feed my baby?

I ask him to leave me alone, and at least he does that for me.

One of the kinder nurses tells me not to worry, she will fix it

226

so I can stay. I should be happy but somehow I find myself crying uncontrollably. I am aching all over. I want to sleep.

Eventually, the doctor turns up with an entourage of pen-pushers. I don't even care what they think of me. I just blurt the whole story out to them: I've been to hell and back in the last week. For your information I helped someone bring in hash from India. I made a very bad mistake. But I am not a drug addict. And surely I have some rights now. My son has rights. We are entitled to medical treatment and I am not leaving this hospital. If you force me out, I will leave here and go straight to the papers, and I will probably pass out in a reporter's arms.

Because I don't care anymore. You cannot hurt me any more.

They let me stay.

11.7.90
I heard the babe cry for the first time &
realised this is only the beginning of all the
pain he will have to endure when they recon-
struct his hand & foot . . .

Spoke to Dr David Thomas today. He assures me
the baby's condition was Bad Luck . . .

You beauty, I'm being transferred to Lismore
tomorrow.

Of course, they try to say that I will have to make my own way up to Lismore while the baby is flown by air ambulance. It is like they are going out of their way to hinder me at every opportunity. Fortunately, the wonderful Dr Thomas comes to the rescue once again and assures me it is standard procedure for mother and child to be flown up together.

The doctor from Westmead has written a letter to Lismore Base Hospital claiming I am well enough not to need to be admitted. But by the time I arrive up north, I am haemorrhaging. The nurse takes one look at me, at the blood all over my clothes and now dripping on the floor, and finds me a bed.

What a relief to have moved closer to home. The hospital at Lismore is so much more relaxed than Sydney; I can actually feel my body begin to recover. I am especially grateful because my friend Rosie is a nurse here and she takes wonderful care of me. She bathes and nurtures me, leaving me with nothing to do but tend to my baby. There is such a strong drive inside me to make him well, with massages and love and breast milk.

I feel that the baby responds to the new environment too. Every day he grows stronger and puts on more weight. The nurse can't believe he was born at thirty-two weeks, he is progressing so well. He is out of the humidicrib, the tube in his nose is gone and he is on full breastfeeds, sucking well. He must have inherited some of his mum's survival skills. The doctor says that with a few more days improvement we will be able to transfer to the little hospital at Byron Bay. Practically home.

For now I can take my baby in my arms and stare in wonder. He looks back and gives me the cutest smile. The silly nurse says it is just wind. Absolute rubbish. He is happy to see me happy. Little one, you have won my heart. What do I call you? I need a strong name with a worthy meaning.

He has blond eyebrows and blond eyelashes. He doesn't have ten fingers and ten toes, but he has the cutest possible personality and the inner strength of an ox. Tears don't come anymore when I talk about his disabilities. The initial shock has faded. Now I don't need sympathy, I just need support. I so much want to keep myself together. It is not the time to dwell on what has happened or what could be; I do not want to risk stress affecting my milk supply. It is hard when I am alone; my head fills up with fears and this spills over into tears. I feel sad for my son that I may lose my appeal and have to go to jail, leaving him behind. Who will love him if the worst happens? But then I remind myself that he needs me now. I cannot spoil this time we have together.

```
15.7.90
Happy Birthday Donna. Big 40.
Oh no, not 40 today. I thought I was going to
be 8 mths pregnant 40 & free. Well I've had babe
& nearly wasn't free. Got a gate pass to go home
for the day. We are going to have a few people
around & have a small party. No tears today
Donna.
```

At last they transfer me to Byron Bay Hospital. It is the last step before home and it feels rejuvenating.

My local doctor comes to see me. I last saw him before I went to Sydney to be sentenced, when he wanted to run some tests. However, he then failed to phone me with the results to let me know that I had a Gardnerella infection. They diagnosed it in St Margaret's and I can't help but wonder if things might have been different had I known about the infection earlier. Is it possible the infection caused my premature labour?

Now my doctor seems nervous — or is that just me projecting? He knows he is in trouble with me. He has known me for years and knows I am not a drug dealer, that I don't take drugs. Now I am feeling really angry, so I say to him, A whole chain of events led up to this and you are part of that chain.

Oh, Donna, no, he says. It's not true.

My baby is going to lose another finger, I say.

Oh no, he's not going to lose any more fingers, it's all right.

He is just pacifying me.

For the next few days I sit staring at my baby's tiny hand as his pinkie turns blacker and blacker. It breaks my heart when he loses that last finger.

I wait for my doctor to return and I hand him the tiny pinkie. I told you it was going to drop off.

As soon as Jessie hears I have been transferred to Byron Bay Hospital, she insists on coming to see me. Jessie and Dylan have been with Robert in Toowoomba and I haven't seen them since I was sentenced, trying to distance them from this nightmare. Now that I am free and the baby is out of his humidicrib, she is on her way.

For the past ten days my mind has been swirling with thoughts of Dylan and Jessie. Especially poor Jessie. What must she be going through? How am I going to tell her and Dylan that the baby is not perfect? I have convinced myself I am going to lose Jessie.

So, when Jessie comes in to the hospital for the weekend I have the baby all wrapped up. I even have mittens on his hands. All you can see is his head. Almost immediately, Jessie says, I want to take his clothes off, Mum.

No, I say, you can't do that, he's too little.

I wanna bath him, Mum.

No, I say, you can't do that either, darling. Maybe tomorrow.

Jessie says she doesn't want to go back to Toowoomba. She tells me, I'm going to stay here with you and the baby – okay, Mum?

I just cry, because I think, Shit, after all this she still wants to be with me. So I say, Yep, you can do that. We can be together.

And I can see the look on her face, like, Wow, Mum's the boss again. Mum can move mountains.

Then she adds, Will you promise me that I can take the baby's clothes off tomorrow, Mum?

We'll see.

Rosie takes Jessie for the night, and when Jessie returns the next morning, the first thing she wants to do is undress the baby.

We're not allowed to take his clothes off, Jessie, I say.

Well, can I play with him?

Sure.

She is a little mother, cuddling him and kissing and cooing, and I can see instant bonding going on. I want her to bond with him without knowing he has a problem.

But, of course, the next day Jessie again wants to bath the baby.

Okay, Jessie, but we need to have a little talk first.

I remove the baby's soft, pale wrap, revealing his damaged hand. And I say, There's a problem, Jessie. He's not very well. We don't know what's wrong with him but he is missing some fingers.

She just says, That's all right, Mum. That's okay.

Yeah?

Yeah, that's all right, Mum, I don't care. I just love him. Can I give him a bottle?

He's breastfed, darling. But maybe you could give him some water.

So she nurses him with a little bottle of water before renewing her pleas to bath the baby.

Jessie, there's another problem.

What is it, Mum?

Well, let's take off his clothes.

We undress his tiny frame and I say, It's his foot.

She looks at it: It's all right, Mum.

God, it tears my heart out. But Jessie just says, I don't care. I love him, Mum.

I underestimated Jessie. I am overjoyed to have my daughter back with me and to watch her fall in love with her baby brother. From that day onwards, there is no shame. Jessie just doesn't care. He is her baby brother and he is okay.

So she baths him and I say, You know, Jess, I think we could probably take him home, what do you think about that?

Yeah!

Harper David Ehrenburg

I've decided to call my son Harper. It has taken some time to name you darling, but I needed to get to know you first and as you will have a name for years to come I want it to be a name that suited you. So Harper it is. Harper you are so beautiful. I . . . love you. I just can't take my eyes off you. You . . . are bringing me joy. After all the pain, I'm feeling pleasure.

CHAPTER 28

27.7.90
Home, so good to be home. Babe Harper has settled in well. Still not crying. Totally at
peace, this little one.

I am back on my verandah at Old Bangalow Road, with my
trees, ocean view, my dog, Ralph, my Jessie and my Harper close
by. I can breastfeed my baby in peace. He is not even five pounds,
so a nurse comes to the house every day to weigh him and we
watch him thrive. Sometimes it is hard to be the strong one, to
be the boss, but Harper and Jessie give me so much pleasure.
And what choice do I have?

Jessie has taken on the role of a mum. Sometimes I express
milk into a bottle and she feeds Harper. She calls herself
Mummy 2.

I have five months of freedom. Five months until my appeal.
The lawyers are going to use my medical condition as the
grounds for their appeal. Even while I have been in hospital I
have been conducting telephone conferences with them, hiring a
new QC, drawing up lists of every house I have ever bought and

sold in this ridiculous routine to have my assets released. If the lawyers did what they were paid to do, the assets would have been cleared long ago. Everything is still frozen, even my car. I literally have no cash, just a pile of IOUs and legal bills. Now the accountants are after me, the tax man is harassing me, and there are medical bills coming in, too. The kids and I are eating and dressing courtesy of a credit card. I know it is only procedure that is delaying the release of my assets – at least there is no worry about that outcome – but this doesn't ease the burden. The minute the court gives me the all clear I will have to sell a house just so I can clear my debts.

I don't understand why, all that time when I was rushing from Byron Bay to Sydney to attend court, pregnant and ill, not once did a lawyer or anyone say to me, Why don't we adjourn this until after you have the baby? There were grounds to do that but no one ever suggested it to me. Had I made it through the pregnancy without all the court worries, there is a chance my child could have been born in a safe environment, healthy and secure. But no one thought to mention it.

I still cry for my son at night. I don't invite people to visit us anymore; we are spending a lot of time alone. Sometimes I just sit and look at the ocean and cry uncontrollably about everything that has happened. I cry because I may yet have to go to jail; cry for Harper, my sweet little boy, for the operations that have yet to come; cry because I may have to leave my baby; cry because I may have to leave Jessica and Dylan. There are days when I just don't get out of bed.

Finally, my assets are released. I love our verdant backyard and water views up in Old Bangalow Road but, with all the debts piling up, I decide the best thing to do is put that place on the market and move us to the corner house I have done up in town. I feel sad letting go of the family home but it makes the most financial sense, and we need to do whatever we can to make sure Harper has the best medical care we can afford. We will plant lots of trees and give the new house a soul of its own.

27.8.90
Harper was due today. He is very aware of what's happening around him. I feel a bit better now, starting to deal with what has happened. Jessie is a great help, she is so attached with Harper & loves him to death. Up every three hours still feeding him & loving him. Everything about me is changing. I'm slowly becoming at peace . . . I'm trying to forgive Eddie as I don't want to become bitter. He has to live with what he has done. Thank you Eddie for giving me Harper.

Harper needs physiotherapy on his damaged hand and foot. Now that he is almost five pounds, I take him down to Sydney for assessment with a paediatric surgeon. We still need to find out why this happened and how we can fix it. Normally, babies are assessed when they are born, but in our case . . . well, in my opinion, my son was discriminated against because I was a prisoner.

Our first stop is the Assessment Clinic at Camperdown Children's Hospital. Geneticist Dr Tony Lipson warmly invites us into his office. He is tall and handsome, and immediately I feel we are in good hands. He just wants to give Harper the best care he can.

Dr Lipson examines Harper, noting down his 'extensive hand and foot deficiencies': the constriction rings, the missing fingers and toes – 'intrauterine amputations' – the toes fused together.

Poor little Harper is only two months old and screams like he has never done before.

Dr Lipson is sure that Harper's injuries occurred in the week before he was born – the week when they were suppressing his birth in St Margaret's – owing to the presence of the healing scabs where his fingers had dropped off. He is convinced the whole thing is directly related to the premature rupture of my membranes.

I suppose I feel relieved. I mean, it is definitely not genetic. But I can feel the anger welling up, all the same. Why was my labour suppressed for so long when it was doing all this damage?

Despite the extent of Harper's disabilities, Dr Lipson is positive. He thinks Harper is absolutely delightful and says, I really think he's going to grow into a fully independent young man.

On my way out, he adds, If you are going to litigate, I suggest you do it now.

From Dr Lipson's office, we head to the Limb Deficiency Clinic, where we meet hand surgeon Dr Michael Tonkin. He wants to operate on Harper, half a finger at a time. He books him in for the first lot of surgery six weeks from now. Dr Tonkin says he will need about ten operations over the coming years. I suddenly feel bombarded by all this medical information, the decisions I have to make. I wish there was someone to be here with me, someone to help me decide what to do.

We have to stay in Sydney a couple more days to attend court; I need to apply to alter my bail conditions so I can travel with Harper for more doctor's appointments.

```
12.9.90
Supreme Court
I go on my own with Harper to vary bail condi-
tion. I stand in front of Judge so&so & I win.
Report twice a week instead of every day. I
```

speak with a quiver in my voice. I try to stop the tears. Moments before I was totally together. I stand in the court room, it's full of men. I feel so intimidated but at the same time I must stand up for myself . . .

What have I learnt by all this? One, never get on the wrong side of the law. 2. Look at the next man I fall in love with. 3. Be at home & love my children. And most of all only Donna can make Donna happy. Harper, I feel so close to you. Being 40 & a mum is so good.

14.9.90
. . . the appeal has been set down on 14th December . . .

[no date]
Back in Byron, now living at [the corner house in town]. I love this house. I like being around people. I want to see them but not talk to them.

I have shut myself off from everyone. I feel so worn down, so sad. And not only that, everyone has heard all these stories about Harper and how he is deformed and disfigured. You know what gossip is like in a small town. So I never take him out publicly, because I don't want anyone projecting a bad feeling onto Harper. When you have a baby, the first thing everyone wants to touch is their hands.

But my good friend up the road, Gwen, is having a birthday party and I decide we should go. It is time we got out. We need friends around us. So I take Harper up to the party.

When we arrive, Gwen asks me to leave. She says she doesn't want Harper to be there. He is only a few months old, but she doesn't want him there because she doesn't want people to know she has a friend who has a baby with no fingers. She actually says that. And then, as if to make it okay, she adds, Donna, it's not your problem, it's my problem.

Well, you can keep that problem all to yourself, I say.

7th Nov.
5 weeks to go before I'm in court again. The nightmares are coming back . . .
Just got news I have to take Harper to Sydney for his first operation. I now must stay strong for him.

It is horrible when you have a baby who has to have an operation. Especially if you are breastfeeding. You are not allowed to feed the baby for hours before, but you are holding him. Your breasts are filling up with milk, and he can smell it, and he is crying, and he is trying to get at your breasts. I do everything I can to hide the milk. I wear a bodice, I express as much as I can, but the more you express, the more it comes in, and I am on my own.

Then I have to hand him over and they anaesthetise him. I stand there while they stick the mask over his face and then he goes limp. Bloody hell. It is just never over.

15th Nov
Harper has now gone to theatre. I take him to the operating room then I'm told to go, it will be 4 hours wait ahead. I just start to cry, no one sees me. I'm all alone. To have to go through this alone is awful. The nurses expect me to take care of everything. I don't mind, it's just that I wish someone else was there for Harper too & to relieve me from time to time. He is in so much pain. Unbelievable pain. He

just screams & screams. I feel for him. Before
when he cried I could always stop his cry by
feeding him or loving & changing him. But this
was a whole new ball game, I just didn't know
what to do other than walk him up & down the
hallway. The nurses ask me to take him out on
the verandah. He was going blue, the pain was
that bad. I can't eat, I can't sleep. I feel
sick with worry. Over & over in my mind I keep
saying it didn't have to happen. It's all very
well for people to say it's going to be OK. They
don't see him every day. They don't see that he
is right handed & he just can't grab with that
hand.

I am sitting with Harper after surgery and he is all bound up,
broad bandages on his battered little body. Then the anaesthetic
starts to wear off and now he is sobbing and vomiting. The
hands are so sensitive. It is such a delicate operation and all his
little nerve endings sear with the agony of it. I just want to cuddle him, feed him, and I can't even do that.

The doctor comes to see us. It seems now he has less of his fingers than I was led to believe. I wonder when I will ever stop
crying. For Harper, this is only the beginning. He has to go
under again in two weeks when they take out the stitches. And
they haven't even begun work on the other hand.

22.11.90
One week after Harper's operation & off to
Sydney again on Wed for yet another operation.
His foot has been bleeding. It looks like he is
trying to separate the toe by stretching out his
toes.

239

Only 20 days left before I know which way my future is going.

28th
Harper's 7th plane trip
Sydney North Shore Hospital

29.11.90
Waiting to go to theatre. So now the nightmare begins. Last nite I'm told Harper was first on the list so they said last feed at 2am. So I argue & said it's too long for Harper so they checked & then said last feed at 3.30 which he had. Then this morning I'm told he is first so I wait. 8am goes by, still he hadn't gone to theatre. So now Harper is screaming screaming. It's so cruel, now they tell me he's not first on the list. My back is killing me, he smells my milk. I have to give him to a nurse to hold. It makes me cross to see Harper this way, all other little babes have another parent to help. It's times like this when the anger sets in about Eddie.

9.55am Harper still screaming. I'm crying, my back is bad. I wish they would get him to surgery. I've never seen him so distressed. My God, this is only his second operation . . .

They have at last come to take Harper to theatre . . .

Harper has just gone to recovery. The dressing is off. The anaesthetist is not as friendly as he was at the last operation, maybe Dr Tonkin has told him my fate & he thinks I'm a terrible person. Just now I feel very flat and overwhelmed by this whole hospital stuff. I'm waiting now for Harper to wake & then I'll take him back to the ward. All they have done is take out stitches. I'm worried about not being covered by medical benefits. I'm outside recovery & I can hear Harper crying. I wish I could be there for him.

6th Dec
Time is running out. I'm losing control. I'm freaking out at Jessica. It's her birthday & she's unhappy. I could snap at any moment. I want to cry, I want to confide in someone but there's no one I feel close enough to. What if I go to jail. What & how do I cope. What do I do. I could explode at any moment. Maybe my last few days left with Harper & Jessie . . .
I have to pay my bills, fix my affairs, do my will.

12th Dec
2am Obviously I can't sleep. I have to be up at 6. Such a long journey tomorrow. From Sydney I have to go to Westmead Hospital for Harper's head ultrasound then a quick night with [friends] before facing the 3 judges on Friday. My head is spinning. I'm wondering who the judges are . . .
    I must choose photos to take. I'm only allowed 6 if I go to jail.

13th Dec
Harper has now been on 9 planes since birth, had
two operations yet nothing seems to bother him.
He sleeps all night & is such a happy go lucky
boy. I couldn't wish for a better child. I hope
we can stay together. I cry as I write this. I
feel so sad. We are landing in Sydney. Now I'm
on my own.

. . . I've been told I have one judge that is
okay, the other 2 are hard & tough.

14.12.90 Supreme Court Day
25th court date
5am I don't think I can go back to sleep, it's
finally going to be over today. It's been one
year since this nightmare started . . .

My Toothless Wonder
He lays in my arms & stares at me & smiles, so
relaxed, so happy. I can't help but think is
this my last day with him. I just don't want to
let him go.

I'm told the judges can make a decision without looking at me or Harper, it's extraordinary
to think they haven't even met me & my future
is in their hands . . .

7am Time is getting near. I'm feeling tired &
strange. I must deep down believe I'm going home
otherwise I just can't believe I could be so
calm. I think I'm going into shock. My jaw is
tight, my back is aching, I can't seem to move.
I'm cemented in this chair. I'm feeding Harper,

giving him as much as he will take, so if the worst happens, at least he will have a full tummy . . .

10am Supreme Court. Three judges walk out into the court all in red gowns.

CHAPTER 29

My case is first on the list. I have a lot of support in court. Friends and lawyers, friends who are lawyers. My appeal is based on a point of law that allows for a circumstance that was present but unknown at the time of sentencing to be introduced as fresh evidence based on its subsequent impact. Which, in my case, is my infection. While I didn't know I had the infection when I was sentenced, we are now hoping the court will allow it in as evidence because of its relevance to everything that has happened to Harper and me since.

My lawyers instruct me to sit behind them and it is then that I start freaking out. This is do or die. I am sobbing. I am uncontrollable. Because any moment now I could be taken off and Harper will instantly be weaned. He is just outside the courtroom door, with Leo Doublecross. But if the three judges throw out my appeal I won't even get to kiss him goodbye. He will go home with Leo and his wife, and I will go straight to jail.

Chief Justice Gleeson, Justice Samuels and Justice Loveday look down on me wearing their wigs and Santa-Claus gowns, surveying their wood-panelled world of law. Justice Loveday begins to talk. He details my case and my 'most unfortunate early life'. Then he goes into Harper's birth and what I went through with Corrective Services.

He says: There is no doubt she underwent severe trauma through all of this. Not only was she in agony throughout the period but she was subjected to the indignity of being hand-cuffed in the ambulance and of Corrective Services staff being present for much of the time. Indeed, they were persuaded to leave the delivery room only for the final stage of birth.

Just then, from outside, Harper lets out an almighty scream and everyone stops. He must want a breastfeed – or maybe Leo has pinched him, I don't know. But it is fantastic, because suddenly everyone in the courtroom realises what is at stake here. What this is all about. There is a real child here who wants his mumma.

Justice Loveday looks at me and explains that this is a most unusual case. He is quoted in the newspaper as saying, It's one of the worst cases, if not the worst case, of personal hardship I have ever seen.

Then he says the words I have been longing to hear: he proposes quashing my sentence and letting me walk out of court with my baby and a good behaviour bond.

Chief Justice Gleeson speaks up: I agree.

Then Justice Samuels: I also agree . . . this is obviously a very tragic and difficult case.

Leo walks into the courtroom and hands Harper to me. Instantly, I nestle my beautiful baby boy into my breast and he starts to feed.

                          Free!!

Harper and I, Leo and his wife, my wonderful barrister, Tony Bellanto, and David Hanlon drink champagne and feast on Chinese food at the Hilton Hotel. I feel elated and so relieved.

Then Harper and I fly north, back to the warm salty air and tropical greenery of Byron Bay, to our family and our rambling wooden home.

EPILOGUE

Harper had eight or ten rounds of surgery before the doctors said he had to undergo psychological testing to see whether he could stand any more pain. Enough, they said. He has had all he can handle.

I wish I had lost my own fingers instead. But, by crikey, he was resilient.

Harper was two by then. I was forty-two, and exhausted. It was time for us to start to heal.

I needed to rebuild my family's unity. I needed to let go of the anger: towards Eddie, the hospital, the guards, the judicial system. I didn't want to be angry anymore, and I didn't want Harper to learn to be angry. What he needed was a strong, healthy mum with an open heart, and tender surroundings and as much love as we could all give him.

I decided to take a ten-year lease on a house in Bali so we could spend the winters there. I chose a lovely thatched-roof home with no walls and a sunken outdoor bath in a compound in Seminyak. It was our retreat, a place where we could be nurtured. To make having the house do-able, I started a business importing antique Indonesian furniture into Australia, and we rented out our home in Byron for the six months of each year that we would be gone.

Every April, as we would step off the plane into the island's frangipani-scented warmth, it was like sinking into a deep, relaxing bath. The anger, the exhaustion and the pain began to dissolve into the steamy air.

We took long swims and walks along the beach; gave our weary bodies over to massages and released our bruised minds to the gentleness of the Balinese people. I learned a lot from watching the Balinese: the way they accept whatever life throws at them, the way they respect and adore children, the way they honour family, and their playful sense of humour. Slowly, I began to absorb those lessons. And Harper, blessed to be embraced by our Balinese friends, inherited a wonderful tapestry of Hindu, Buddhist and Australian values.

I am proud to say that Harper has grown into a very talented and unique young man. At fifteen he has travelled through Asia and Europe, and even attended school in the south of France. He speaks fluent French, and is currently nagging me for Indonesian lessons.

He is a cerebral kid. He wants to be a writer and always has his head in a book. At the moment he is reading *The Hitchhiker's Guide to the Galaxy*.

He's not into sport so much, although he did join the soccer team once. He would go off to the games, telling me not to bother coming to watch him. One day when I decided to turn up anyway, I couldn't find him on the pitch.

I spotted him under a tree, reading.

Harper, you're supposed to be playing soccer.

Mum, there's a lot of kids in the team. They don't need me. I'm educating myself.

He can be a manipulative little bugger, Lord love him.

Harper manages well with his disability. Even now he still

needs surgery, but he can use his hand to do most things. Not that it hasn't been hard for him. Even though he seems okay, I really feel he has suffered at school. He has been humiliated by other children, laughed at and bullied, because of his disability. Each time he starts a new school or goes to shake someone's hand, my heart breaks. He has to deal with this every day. I will never forgive myself for that; I will take it to my death.

I suppose Harper has dealt with the bullying by going into a corner with his book. And I have always stood up for him. I think he feels good about that; I am the iron lady. If there is a problem, Mum will sort it out. But more than that, Harper is wonderfully philosophical; accepting and compassionate. He has never retaliated. He is a little Buddhist. He has an altar in his bedroom with his statue of Buddha where he makes offerings of rice and flowers. It is something he has chosen to do on his own. I think part of it comes from spending so much time in Bali and maybe being a Cancerian, but it is also just his nature. He is extremely caring and understanding.

I am in the process of telling Harper the story surrounding his birth. It is difficult, but bit by bit I am revealing it to him. He is very inquisitive and he has big ears when he is supposed to be asleep.

I have resisted telling him until now because I knew he would cry. Not for himself. He would cry for me. That's what Harper is like.

Eddie is not involved in Harper's life, although we did see him again. We were in Bali and Harper was two. Harper was off with friends and I was in a restaurant having breakfast. I was just about to take a bite of my fruit salad when I looked up into the large mirror on the wall in front of me and saw Eddie's reflection. I couldn't believe it. I hadn't seen him since I was pregnant.

Eddie was looking at his bare chest in the mirror, doing his hair. I thought, God, wouldn't it be fabulous if that song 'You're So Vain' came on now. If my life were a movie, that's what would happen.

For a long while, Eddie didn't notice that I was watching him, but I kept my eyes on him until finally he looked up.

He jumped up as though he wanted to run. I think he thought he might be arrested or something. Maybe he thought I would attack him. You could see the panic in him.

But I was much calmer now. I knew I was okay, and the last thing I needed was a fresh bout of anger and resentment. So I approached him and said, You don't have to run, Eddie. Your son is here if you would like to meet him.

We met up later on the beach, and I introduced father and son. I think Eddie was waiting for the bomb to drop. He couldn't believe I wasn't going ballistic. But the way I saw it was, he had made a choice to destroy his child and me in order that he could be saved. If he had owned up to the truth, who knows how events might have turned out? But the thing is, he has to live with what he's done for the rest of his life. Which makes his problem far worse than mine.

I said that to him. I also said, I might have an issue with you, but that doesn't mean you should have an issue with Harper. I have vowed never to turn Harper against you.

I let Eddie take Harper for a swim in the surf and I stood on the sand videotaping them. Afterwards, Eddie gave me US$700. I think it was out of guilt. I think for the first time he actually felt sorry because he could see what we had been through; what had been at stake.

We saw Eddie only once more after that, a year or so later back in Bali.

Harper came in from swimming and said, Mum, my dad's out there. Can I go with my dad?

Harper was about three at the time. So I said okay and asked the Balinese nanny to take him around to Eddie's house for dinner as I didn't want to see him.

Harper returned an hour later, devastated. My dad says it wasn't the right time to have dinner with him now. He changed his mind.

Harper went upstairs, lay on his bed and sobbed. I never heard a child cry with such intensity. He was broken-hearted. I was beside myself. Because all this time I had been protecting Harper from his father, and in one unguarded moment he did this to him.

We have never seen him again. I told Eddie, You are never going to get the opportunity to hurt my son again.

I said to Harper, I'm sorry about your father, darling. He's just a silly man. He's a lot younger than me and he knows that I am so strong I can do the job of both parents. I'm your Mummy and Daddy in one. I'll do everything for you. If you want me to kick a football, I will. If you want to wrestle, I will.

Now Harper is a bit older he's not as interested in his dad. I have heard him explain to people, My dad's not much of a dad. I say to him, You're lucky, Harper, I didn't have a mum or a dad.

Over the years, Harper has occasionally asked, Where's my dad? And I say, He's in India doing primal therapy.

That is not an attack, it's true. He is in India searching for himself. With gurus. What a luxury. But what he doesn't realise is that your guru is right in front of you. Your guru is your family.

While I was writing this book, Harper was given his own autobiographical assignment. His Year 9 English teacher asked the class to write about a defining moment in their life. I was so proud of Harper's story that I asked him if I could share it with you. Perhaps it is the start of his writing career.

TRUE STORY By Harper Ehrenburg

Sometimes I get angry and wonder, 'Why the hell did it happen to me, out of all the people in the world?' I get back to my senses and say, 'There are billions of people who are missing an arm, a leg, a couple of digits, and if they all started to cry every time they thought about their missing limb, we're not yet out of the barn' (as the French say, which means the problem is not yet over). *On est pas encore sortie de l'auberge.*

When you are little your mum tells you a stork dropped you at the doorstep. Yeah right! Well, my mum told me she bought me at Woolies at low price (the manufacturer had got it wrong for the first model) . . .

Every time somebody asked me about my fingers, I would tell them it was medical malpractice and it was a long story. I didn't know what it meant but it got the adults to quieten down. The kids on the other hand, I needed to invent some weird story about crocodiles biting them off to stop the kids babbling on about it.

The doctor in charge of my birth did not want to work on a mother under seven months pregnant. (My mum was 31 weeks.) So my mother was put on a drug to stop the labour. In the meantime my mother's womb tore and bits of fibre were coiling around my fingers and toes like a tourniquet. When my mother was finally allowed to go through labour they only had time to save my thumb. My other fingers resemble little but stumps.

As I grew older I started to realise how much my disability affected me, as in getting girlfriends, or my friends being affected by a little joke I made about my fingers . . . My mother has done everything she can to stop negative energy coming towards me. She's taken me to Bali, to France, to India and even Japan just to escape the morality of the Australian system.

As I am writing she tells me her faith has been restored. 80% of the people that we meet are positive and encouraging about my disability. (Most people don't even notice my hand – they must be foreigners. Only foreigners and people from 3rd world countries are so uninterested in your physical form.)

It doesn't matter! My disability doesn't affect me as much as when I was young.

When I ask Harper, How's your life been? What sort of life have you lived? he always says he has had a happy life.

Harper and I have filled our overgrown garden in Byron Bay with tropical flowers and Balinese sculpture to remind us of our Indonesian haven. Each day I wake up and take our little dog, Jet-Set, down to the organic bakers to buy fresh bread for breakfast, then come back and get Harper ready for school. In the afternoons I head to the beach for a swim.

Living in such a lovely spot, we have a constant trail of friends up from the southern states. There is always someone interesting to talk to and these people have become our extended family. I run my own little orphanage, only it is warm and pretty and serene.

It has been a tough ride but I turned out all right. I raised three kids and did a good job. Dylan has lived overseas, worked as a circus acrobat, and is now in Sydney with his gorgeous girl-friend concentrating on his acting career, while Jessie has modelled around the world, studied journalism, and been a dive instructor up in Queensland.

I still think of Wayne all the time – that poor child. I believe he lives in Melbourne somewhere. He was born in 1968; I could be a grandmother by now. It is only a matter of making a phone call and I could speak to him but I am too scared. I contacted his father, Graeme, twenty-odd years ago, hoping to find out how Wayne was, what he was like, but it was awkward between us and I didn't learn very much. I even dialled Wayne's grandmother's old number as recently as last year but hung up when somebody answered.

It is only now I am in my fifties that I have been able to confront my past; drag out the Welfare files and medical records that have been hidden in my bottom drawer for twenty-odd years. Maybe I am looking to resolve issues. Searching for identity. Is this what you do at my age? Take stock?

Looking back through the files and the diaries that I have kept hidden for so long has been a good thing. I believe you have to make peace with your past and move on. It took a long time for me to deal with all this. I think I must have had depression, or post-traumatic stress disorder. But I am strong now, and have a fantastic circle of friends and family around me, including my half-siblings, Betty and Warren. And even though I never really formed a bond with the others, we speak too. Maybe now I can close the book.

Who knows where I will go next? I think I am a bit of a gypsy. But I don't want to talk about how tragic my life has been, because now when I assess it I see it has been great. Look at where I am right now. I am in full control of my destiny. I have a beautiful home in Byron Bay. What's more, I have my very own family – my three incredible children – who I love beyond the moon and the stars. And they are three good kids, too, with good values.

I couldn't ask for more than that.

A NOTE FROM DONNA

People often ask me why I did not litigate over Harper's injuries. To be honest, for a while I was in two minds about it.

In my heart, I really believe Harper's medical care in the weeks before and after his birth was compromised because I was in hospital under prison guard. Of course, it was. I was a second-class citizen and that is how I was treated. I had given birth before. I knew how well the midwives usually took care of you.

The words of the geneticist, Tony Lipson, would often come back to me: *If you are going to litigate, I suggest you do it now.* Dr Lipson must have thought we had a case because his report stated that Harper's deformities occurred in the week before birth. That was the week I was in St Margaret's Hospital doped up on Ventolin in order to keep my baby from being born.

There is no doubt in my mind that the main reason everyone wanted to suppress my labour was because Corrective Services wanted me moved closer to the jail, when it would have made more sense to move me to the nearby Royal Women's or King George V hospitals. I am convinced that had I been hospitalised under different circumstances, my child would have been delivered before things went so terribly wrong.

With all that in mind I did some research to back up my gut feeling. I applied for medical records and enlisted specialists to review the files. I arranged for a clinical nurse consultant from St Vincent's Hospital in Lismore, a man named David Tibby, to look through my files. He has been nursing for over thirty years and wrote a report documenting the flaws in our treatment.

He noted that at no time did any medical staff talk to me about the risks to my unborn child, or inform me of the likely outcomes of suppressing my labour. Which, he points out, is contrary to Australian health care policy. I know how alone and vulnerable I felt at the time. I was powerless, both because I was so shaky from the drugs and because the doctors communicated with the guards about my condition, rather than speaking to me. At no time was I aware there was a chance my baby was in distress. No one mentioned it to me.

Secondly, David Tibby's report reiterated my belief that the desire to have me transferred to Westmead was the primary consideration above and beyond my health and that of my unborn child, which resulted, he says, in 'injudicious use of Ventolin' to suppress my labour and transfer me.

More damningly, though, Tibby pointed out that Ventolin is not supposed to be used when there is foetal distress (the baby's heart rate, together with the queries in my file that I was possibly leaking meconium, were both indications that the baby could have been in distress). Neither, he wrote, is Ventolin supposed to be used when there is active uterine bleeding, or where rupture of the membranes and a suspected infection in the membranes is present. 'The records in Westmead conclude that all three factors had occurred,' he wrote. So, basically, what he was saying is that I should never have been on Ventolin at all.

He concluded: 'Donna's overall healthcare management was definitely affected by her [incarceration] and the presence of the Corrective Services. The obvious prevailing objective was to suppress her labour and move her as soon as possible. Donna's unrelenting labour prevented this on several occasions, despite extremely high doses of Ventolin and the fact she showed obvious signs of overdose . . .

'I believe close examination of Donna Ehrenburg's notes show less than satisfactory healthcare management and show a failure in the Duty of Care to Harper.'

So, it seems Tibby thought Harper's injuries could have been the result of bad management at St Margaret's. I believe it, too.

I went to see a nurse at St Margaret's who was especially kind to me while I was in hospital. She said that what I was put through was inhuman. She told me she believed I should have had the emergency Caesarean that I was prepped for, but a phone call came through ordering that it be stopped. It is not hard to guess where that call came from.

I also sought out the opinions of experts in the field of obstetrics. One well-known professor told me, Donna, sure it is better to keep a baby of thirty-one weeks in the womb. But I can give you three good reasons why that baby should have been delivered immediately. For a start, he was big enough to be born. Secondly, you were losing green fluid. And thirdly, the baby was obviously in distress. And, he added, if you want to sue, you only need a balance of probability and you have won the case.

I decided to phone the young obstetrician who treated me at St Margaret's Hospital, Dr Betty Liounis, and tell her I was contemplating legal action against Corrective Services. She said she totally supported me; she found Corrective Services difficult to work with and said their disorganisation was 'reprehensible'.

She remembered being mad with them because the medical staff were constantly kept waiting for decisions to come through from Corrective Services bosses. 'You couldn't get any right or wrong answers,' she said.

Dr Liounis also confirmed my belief that it was Corrective Services pushing to get me to Westmead. 'They weren't happy having you at St Margaret's,' she said, adding that the logical solution would have been to send me to the Royal Women's or King George V hospitals. There was a financial issue involved in moving me to Westmead, she said. All that overtime was adding up.

This is all the proof I need that my child's best interests were not the priority in the week before his birth. Sure, obstetrics is not a black-and-white science. With Harper still in my womb, there were a lot of unknowns. Perhaps he would have suffered his injuries anyway. I could accept that, had I known that he had been given the best treatment possible. But he wasn't. The involvement of Corrective Services clearly affected his medical treatment.

Dr Liounis agreed. 'Your situation would have been very different [had you not been under guard]. There wouldn't have been procrastination in delivery. Decisions would have been a lot firmer . . . it did interfere with your management, we all felt it . . . of course we all felt it.'

With all of this swirling through my head, the anger welled up inside me. This didn't have to happen to my child. So I hired a lawyer and told him I wanted to sue Corrective Services and St Margaret's Hospital: the hospital for suppressing my labour unnecessarily, and Corrective Services for all their bullying, humiliation, and for interfering in my son's treatment. I felt I needed to do it for Harper.

But in the end, I just couldn't go through with it. Every time I tried to dredge it all up, the nightmares returned. I couldn't sleep. I cried all the time for no reason. Not for me, but for my son, what he had had to go through. He was just a little baby.

I realised that I needed to leave that behind me. Move on. I needed to be strong for Jessie and Dylan and Harper, heal my family. I wanted to be a good mum. So I fought off the depression. Some days it was like I was on stage in front of my children. I fed the baby, nice and calm, tucked them all into bed and kissed them goodnight. Then I would sob.

Slowly, it started to become less of an act. Eventually, I could feel myself begin to heal.

While I couldn't bring myself to go through with a damages suit, with all this damning material at my fingertips, I felt as though I had to do something. At the very least, I needed someone to acknowledge what I had been through, what Harper was yet to go through. Perhaps we could implement change. So I made formal complaints against St Margaret's Hospital and the Department of Corrective Services.

Over many months all my complaints were investigated but the findings were not what I had hoped for. Essentially, the Health Care Complaints Commission (HCCC) disregarded my complaints, only allowing that the communication between the medical staff and myself was not adequate. Now, there's an understatement.

I only realise now that there was no point in having a complaint about the Health Department investigated by the Health Department. It's not really an independent inquiry, is it? But it wasn't until I received all the documentation from their internal investigations, that I understood how much of a joke it was.

Parts of the report described the guards as pleasant, and how they were unobtrusive in patient management. It was a world away from my experiences, and from the honest responses I'd been given by caring and humane doctors like the St Margaret's obstetrician Dr Betty Liounis, who had previously admitted to me that my case 'would have been very different. There wouldn't have been procrastination in delivery,' were it not for the involvement of Corrective Services, and that 'It did interfere with your management, we all felt it.'

The Department of Health should not be run by the bureaucrats. It should be run by an independent organisation.

I was happier with the Ombudsman's investigation into the guards. It didn't go so far as to admit that Corrective Services interfered with my health care, but the department did offer me an apology for any hurtful comments the guards might have made.

More importantly, however, the Ombudsman found that there were glaring flaws in the procedure for guards working in hospitals, and instructed Westmead and Corrective Services to negotiate for an improved procedure. Along with rules banning the use of handcuffs during labour, and preserving privacy during childbirth, the new procedures that were put into practice as a result of my complaints included the instruction: 'Escorting Officers are to endeavour, in every way, to preserve the dignity of the individual who, during their time at the hospital or medical facility, is firstly a person, secondly a patient and thirdly an inmate.'

It was a small win, but an important one. I felt I had done the right thing, but, more importantly, for me it was over. At last I could bundle up the medical records, legal correspondence, written complaints and my little red journal and file it all away.

Some of it went in the bottom drawer, the rest in a beautiful old Balinese chest. I took a deep breath and heaved the heavy teak box downstairs to store under my house. The cool, damp air felt refreshing.

ACKNOWLEDGEMENTS

Love and thanks to all my family for their constant love and support. To Dylan, for always being there and never judging me; to Jessica, for her advice – I feel that we understand each other more now; and to Wayne – I'm always thinking about you, and sending you my love and well wishes.

My dearest Harper, you have helped me 'put the flesh into the skeleton'. You are my inspiration; you have helped me more than you will know. I know you understand that I only want everyone to know the truth, and I am grateful for your empathy and encouragement.

To Kenny, whom I love dearly – you are so gentle and beautiful, and I just wish that we had spent more time together as brother and sister.

Robert, thank you for giving me two beautiful children – you gave me twelve years of stability that I've somehow never really been able to regain, and I appreciate the love you once had for me.

Finally, to Hana (who hopefully will become part of my family), thank you for your patience and love.

To all of my friends, I am grateful for your encouragement and for enduring my moments of madness, insecurity and vulnerability during the whole ordeal of writing this book.

To my oldest and dearest friend, Rosie Pittman – our lives have been connected for so many years, and we have been there for each other through all kinds of joy and pain. You've shown me how to have fun again – thank you.

To wonderful Faith – you have been by my side throughout everything. Not only do you provide me with your namesake, you have a calming effect on me and I am indebted to you for the trust we have between us. We have so much fun together, and I really appreciate your presence and honesty.

To Sanndy Star, whom I frolicked with at Aquarius, we have known each other for many years – thanks for being a great friend and for being there for me.

To Aldis and Marie, my City girls – thank you for your continued support and advice.

Finally, to my verdant friend Ian – thanks for your understanding and consideration.

I am also thankful to Rob Hampshire for listening to me and dropping everything at a moment's notice to get me through difficult times.

Thank you, Tom Gilliatt, for treating me well and having confidence in my ability to write this book. Thank you, Amy, for helping me with my story; I appreciate all your time and effort.

Donna Davis

I would like to thank Robin Barker and Anne Grundy for their incredible generosity of time and expertise in agreeing to read the manuscript; your advice was greatly appreciated. Also, a huge thanks to the wonderful team at Pan Macmillan, in particular, publisher extraordinaire Tom Gilliatt and our exceptionally patient editor, Sarina Rowell.

Amy Willesee